# FINANCIAL FREEDOM

FOR THE

# SALARIED

A Practical Guide to Money Management and Wealth Building

**PAYCHECK TO POWER**

BALRAM CHAUDHARY

## Disclaimers

- The views expressed in the book are the author's own and not the views of the Reserve Bank of India.
- The results and findings in this book are based on data available in the public domain and on stated assumptions. Actual returns, interest rates, tax rules, and market conditions may differ.
- This book is for general educational purposes only and does not constitute financial, investment, tax, or legal advice. Please consult a qualified professional before making any financial decision.

## Free Resources

The templates, trackers, and calculators used throughout this book are available to download free at www.balramchaudhary.com or scan the QR code given below.

***Dedicated to every salaried individual who aspires to attain financial freedom***

Balram Chaudhary

# Table Contents

*Foreword* *i*

*Who Should Read This Book* *iv*

*How to Read This Book for Maximum Benefit* *viii*

1. Introduction - The day I realized I was late 1

2. **The Seven Money Myths That Keep Salaried People Poor** 11

3. Real Struggles of Salaried Persons 36

4. From Reaction to Design 52

5. **The 3-Step Wealth Framework for Salaried Persons** 65

6. **Step One - Protect: Building the Financial Foundation** 76

    *Term Insurance Requirement Worksheet* *98*

    *Health Insurance Requirement Worksheet* *103*

    *Emergency Fund Requirement Worksheet* *107*

7. **Step Two - Invest Systematically: Turning Salary into a Wealth Machine** 110

    *The Four-Account System Model* *113*

    *The Salary-to-Wealth Conversion Model* *127*

    *Monthly Income & Investment Composition Worksheet* *132*

    *Goal Planning & Investment Worksheet* *135*

    *Inflation Adjusted Value Worksheet* *139*

8. **Step Three - Multiply Through Compounding and Discipline** 142

9. How to Apply: From Knowledge to Execution 167

*The 30-Day Financial Reset Plan* *168*

*30-Day Financial Reset Checklist* *175*

*12-Month Financial Progress Tracker* *184*

10. Method to Make ₹100 Crore through Salary - A Case Study 185

*The 5-Year Compounding Hack* *195*

*A Message to 30–45 Year Old Professionals* *196*

11. The Middle-Class Money Trap 199

***Acknowledgements*** ***208***

# Foreword

As a B-School Professor, one of my greatest privileges is seeing students build successful careers after they leave the classroom. Over the years, I have taught and mentored thousands of students who now work in banks, financial institutions, multinational companies, government organizations, and start their own businesses. Watching their professional and financial journeys has taught me something important: earning **a high salary does not guarantee wealth, and wealth is not just for those with the highest incomes.**

Many of my former students have done well in their careers and earn good salaries. Still, I have noticed that career success and financial success do not always go together. Some people with high incomes find it hard to build real wealth because they do not plan their finances well, spend more as they earn more, or start investing too late. On the other hand, I have seen people with modest incomes build significant wealth by being disciplined, patient, and investing regularly.

To me, this shows a big gap in our education system. We spend years teaching students how to get qualifications, find jobs, and earn more. But we rarely teach them how to manage money, build assets, invest wisely, or create long-term wealth. Because of this, many well-educated professionals know how to earn money, but not how to turn their income into financial freedom.

What I like most about this book is its practical and organized approach. Balram understands that for most people, salary is their main source of income, so financial freedom needs to be built step by step from that salary. The book introduces a simple but powerful **Three-Step Financial Freedom Model: Protect, Invest, and Compound**. This framework gives salaried people a clear plan to protect their finances, invest regularly, and use the power of compounding to build long-term wealth.

Unlike many personal finance books that focus on theory, this book puts a strong focus on taking action. With practical examples, worksheets, calculators, and clear advice, Balram encourages readers to go beyond just learning and actually take steps toward financial independence. The book reminds us that financial freedom does not come from luck, guessing, or a huge income. It comes from making smart choices, building good habits, and staying consistent over time.

I have known Balram Chaudhary since his MBA days from 2007-2009. He was a sincere, disciplined, and strong student who always wanted to learn more than what was taught in class. It is great to see that these same qualities still guide him in his work and life. His passion for financial literacy and wealth creation shines through in this book.

Whether you are getting your first salary, are mid-career, or planning for retirement, this book gives useful insights and a practical plan for financial independence. Most importantly, it reminds us that **financial freedom is not just for a lucky few. Anyone with a salary can achieve it by following the right steps with discipline and patience.**

I congratulate Balram on this thoughtful effort to improve financial literacy and help people take charge of their financial future. I am sure this book will inspire many readers to turn their salary into lasting wealth and reach real financial freedom.

**Prof. (Dr) Vivek Ranga**
**Head - Campus Operations**
**Queens University Belfast, GIFT City Campus, India**

# Who Should Read This Book

This book is primarily written for salaried individuals.

It is for people who wake up every morning, go to office, work hard throughout the month, and wait for salary credit messages at the end of the month. It is for employees who are trying to balance dreams, responsibilities, EMIs, family expectations, and an uncertain financial future.

If you are someone who depends largely on a monthly salary, this book is written for you.

But this book is not only for people who are already deep into their careers. In fact, some of the people who may benefit the most from this book are those who are standing at the beginning of their professional journey.

If you are in the final years of your college degree and are about to enter the corporate world, this book can save you from making financial mistakes that silently destroy years of wealth creation.

Most students spend years learning technical skills, engineering concepts, coding languages, management theories, law, medicine, or commerce — but almost nobody teaches them how to manage their salary once they start earning.

Nobody teaches:

- how to handle the first salary,
- how to avoid lifestyle inflation,
- how to start investing early,
- how to use compounding,
- how to choose insurance wisely,
- or how to build long-term wealth systematically.

As a result, many young professionals enter the workforce financially blind.

The first few years of salary often become "enjoyment years." Expensive phones, unnecessary shopping, frequent dining out, impulsive trips, gadgets, and social pressure quietly consume the most powerful years of compounding.

The tragedy is not spending money.

The tragedy is not understanding the cost of delaying investment.

This book is written so that you do not realize this mistake after ten years.

If you are a newly employed professional, this book will help you build the right financial foundation from the beginning itself. The habits formed during the first five years of earning often decide the financial condition of the next thirty years.

This book is especially useful for:

- Young professionals starting their first job
- Employees in private sector jobs
- Government employees
- Middle-class salaried families
- Working professionals struggling with savings discipline
- Individuals confused about investment and insurance products
- Professionals trapped in EMI cycles
- People who earn reasonably well but still feel financially insecure
- Employees who want financial freedom instead of lifelong financial stress

Even experienced salaried individuals in their thirties and forties may discover that despite years of hard work, they have not built meaningful wealth because nobody explained money management in a practical and structured way.

This book attempts to bridge that gap.

This is not a book promising overnight riches.

It is not a trading manual.

It is not a shortcut to luxury.

It is a practical guide for ordinary salaried individuals who want to achieve extraordinary financial stability through discipline, systematic investing, protection planning, and the power of compounding.

The principles discussed in this book are intentionally simple because financial freedom itself is simple — but consistency is difficult.

If you are willing to think long-term, control emotional spending, and systematically convert salary into assets, this book can genuinely change your financial future.

Whether you are about to receive your first salary or are already fifteen years into your career, one truth remains the same:

The earlier you understand money, the easier your life becomes later.

This book is written to help you understand that truth before time teaches it painfully.

# How to Read This Book for Maximum Benefit

This book is not meant to be "finished." It is meant to be implemented.

Most people read personal finance books the same way they watch motivational videos — they feel inspired temporarily, but their financial life remains unchanged. They underline a few lines, feel motivated for two days, and then return to old habits. Months later, nothing improves except their collection of financial books.

Do not make that mistake with this book.

The real value of this book lies not in reading it quickly, but in applying it slowly and honestly to your own financial life.

## Read This Book Like a Personal Financial Audit

While reading every chapter, do not think about "people in general." Think about yourself.

Whenever you read about:

- overspending,

- delaying investments,
- insurance mistakes,
- EMI pressure,
- lifestyle inflation,
- lack of savings, or
- financial stress,

pause and ask yourself:

"Am I doing this?" Note down the mistakes you have made or are still making.

This book will help you the most when you stop reading it as theory and start treating it as a mirror.

Some chapters may make you uncomfortable. That discomfort is valuable. Financial growth often begins when a person honestly accepts their financial mistakes.

## Keep Your Financial Information Beside You

Do not read this book empty-handed.

Keep the following with you while reading:

- salary details,
- monthly expenses,
- bank statements,

- loan details,
- SIP statements,
- insurance policies, and
- approximate household expenses.

Why?

Because this book is practical. Almost every major concept discussed here can be directly applied to your own financial situation immediately.

When you read about emergency funds, calculate your own emergency fund.

When you read about insurance, check whether your current insurance is actually sufficient.

When you read about investments, compare the concepts with your current portfolio.

Reading alone creates awareness.

Calculation creates clarity.

## Use Every Calculator and Worksheet

This is extremely important.

Many readers skip worksheets and calculators because they feel “too basic” or “too time-consuming.” That is a serious mistake.

The calculators in this book are among its most important sections because they convert financial ideas into measurable reality.

A person who says:
“I think my savings are okay”
is financially confused.

A person who calculates:
“My emergency fund requirement is ₹6 lakh”
has financial clarity.

This book contains calculators and worksheets for:

- emergency funds,
- life insurance requirement,
- health insurance requirement,
- investment planning,
- inflation-adjusted goals,
- income allocation, and
- long-term wealth creation.

Use them carefully.

Do not estimate casually. Use real numbers from your own life.

The purpose of these tools is not mathematics. The purpose is awareness.

Many salaried individuals are financially stressed not because they earn less, but because they never calculate where they actually stand.

## Read in Sequence — Do Not Jump Directly to Investing

One of the biggest mistakes readers make is directly jumping to investing chapter and do not read the initial chapters.

People naturally get excited about "making money."

But wealth creation without financial structure is dangerous.

That is why this book follows a deliberate sequence:

1. Understanding financial mistakes
2. Breaking money myths
3. Building financial protection
4. Creating financial systems
5. Investing systematically
6. Using compounding effectively

7. Executing consistently

If you skip the foundation, you may build investments without building financial stability. This is similar to constructing the top floor of a building before creating the base.

Protection comes before multiplication.

## Read Slowly and Pause Frequently

This book is not designed for speed reading.

Some chapters may appear simple at first glance, but their long-term impact is enormous if implemented correctly.

For example:

- starting investments five years earlier,
- increasing SIPs gradually,
- buying proper term insurance,
- avoiding unnecessary EMIs, or
- understanding inflation,

may look like "small ideas," but over 20–30 years they completely change financial outcomes.

Read a chapter.

Pause.

Think about your own life.

Then continue.

Financial freedom is built through understanding, not through page count.

## Implement One Concept at a Time

Do not try to transform your entire financial life in one weekend.

That usually creates confusion and mental exhaustion.

Instead, focus on the four-week plan given in this book. .

## Revisit Important Chapters Again

This is not a book that you should read once and then forget. Your financial life keeps changing with time. Your salary increases, responsibilities grow, expenses rise, goals evolve, and new financial challenges appear at every stage of life. A chapter that may not feel very important today may become extremely relevant five years later.

Therefore, revisit this book periodically. Return to the calculators, worksheets, and financial frameworks again and again. Recalculate your goals, review your insurance coverage, reassess your investments, and honestly evaluate whether you are still following the financial path you originally decided for yourself.

## Discuss the Book with Your Family

Financial stress affects entire families, not individuals alone. Therefore, do not keep financial learning limited only to yourself.

Discuss important ideas from this book with:

- your spouse,
- parents,
- siblings, or
- even close friends.

Many middle-class families suffer financially because money discussions never happen openly.

A financially aware family makes better decisions collectively.

## Most Important: Start Before You Feel Fully Ready

Many readers delay action because they believe they need:

- a higher salary,
- more knowledge,
- perfect timing, or
- complete confidence.

That mindset silently destroys years of compounding.

The perfect time to begin financial discipline never arrives automatically. People who build wealth are not people who know everything.

They are people who start early and remain consistent.

Even a small SIP started today is more powerful than a large investment delayed for years.

## A Final Thought

As you read this book, do not focus on how many chapters you complete.

Focus on how many financial mistakes you avoid.

Do not ask:
"How fast can I finish this book?"

Ask:
"How deeply can I apply this book?"

Because ultimately, this book is not about increasing financial knowledge.

It is about reducing future financial regret.

And that change begins the moment you start implementing what you read.

# Chapter 1

# Introduction - The day I realized I was late

I started earning at the age of 24.

Like most young professionals, I felt proud, independent, and unstoppable. That first salary was more than just money—it was FREEDOM. For the first time, I didn't have to ask my parents for pocket money. I could buy what I wanted without offering explanations. It felt like adulthood had truly begun.

This was my first job. I had just entered the corporate world. I told myself that these were my "enjoyment years." After all, I had spent my college days counting every rupee. I had foregone small desires because I did not want to burden my parents. Now that I was earning, I felt there was no guilt in spending.

I bought clothes I did not really need. I upgraded to the most expensive mobile available in the market. I went out for dinner regularly. I purchased gadgets simply because I could buy them.

Every month, when the salary was credited, I felt rich. And by the end of the month, I would be back to feeling ordinary.

I never imagined investing even a single paisa.

The idea of mutual funds, compounding, insurance planning, and asset allocation—none of this crossed my mind. I believed saving was something serious people did after 35. I believed investing was for people who had "excess money."

Months became years. My income increased gradually. My lifestyle expenses increased faster. I convinced myself that once I earned "enough," I would begin saving properly.

That day never came.

> At 25, I said, "*Let me enjoy one more year.*"
>
> At 27, I said, "*I'll start when my salary doubles.*"
>
> At 29, I said, "*Next year I'll get serious.*"

Then came the moment that changed everything.

## The Conversation That Shook Me

I was about 30 when I met my old friend, Pawan. We had started our careers at roughly the same time. We had similar educational backgrounds. We had similar salaries in the early years.

While catching up, the conversation naturally moved toward work, life, and finances.

Casually, Pawan mentioned that his mutual fund investments had grown to around ₹25 lakh.

₹25 lakh.

I froze.

I thought I had heard him wrong.

"How much?" I asked again.

He smiled and repeated it calmly.

At that moment, something shifted inside me.

I tried to calculate quickly in my mind. We had started earning almost together. Our salaries were similar in the beginning. Yet I had barely saved anything significant. My money had disappeared into lifestyle upgrades and temporary pleasures.

His money had grown quietly into something tangible.

I felt a mix of shock, disbelief, and guilt.

The shirts I bought were gone. The gadgets I upgraded became obsolete. The dinners and weekend expenses were forgotten.

But Pawan had something permanent. A growing net worth. A financial cushion. A sense of control.

While discussing further, he told me something that hit me harder than the ₹25 lakh number.

He said, "Even if my mutual fund corpus grows at just 12% per year, that's ₹3 lakh annually. That's ₹25,000 per month—without doing anything extra."

₹25,000 per month.

Passive.

That was almost half of what I used to earn in my first job.

In that moment, I understood the difference between earning money and building wealth.

## Temporary Happiness vs Permanent Progress

I had spent my hard-earned money on items that did not last even a year. The happiness was instant—but transitory. The satisfaction faded quickly, and I needed another purchase to recreate that excitement.

Pawan, on the other hand, had built something that gave him permanent satisfaction. He had created a foundation. A financial base. A structure that would continue growing whether he bought new clothes or not.

That was the day I began asking uncomfortable questions:

> ***Why weren't we taught this in school?***
> ***Why did I never think about investing from day one?***
> ***Why did I believe saving was something to start "later"?***

The truth was simple: I did not understand the power of compounding.

At 24, I had time in abundance. At 30, I had regret.

And regret is expensive.

## The Cost of Waiting

When you are 24 and single, your financial responsibilities are minimal. Your expenses are under control. You have flexibility. You have fewer commitments.

If you do not start saving and investing during this phase, it becomes harder later.

Once you get married, responsibilities increase. Once you have children, expenses multiply. Once you take a home loan, EMIs consume your freedom.

Each new responsibility demands more money.

If you delay investing until after marriage, you will struggle.
If you delay until after children, you will struggle more.

Time lost in your twenties is difficult to recover in your thirties.

I realized that wealth is not built by earning more. It is built by starting early.

## My Turning Point

After that conversation with Pawan, I could not sleep peacefully for days. Not because I envied him—but because I realized I had wasted a powerful opportunity.

I felt shattered. I felt like a loser. It felt as if I had burned my entire earnings — and six precious years of time.

But guilt alone changes nothing.

Action does.

I read several books on investment, wealth creation, and financial freedom. I began reading about mutual funds. I understood SIPs. I studied compounding. I reviewed my expenses honestly.

And I discovered something even more painful.

I had little understanding of insurance and investment.
I had ignored term insurance.
I had underestimated health insurance.
I had no clear retirement plan.
I was financially active—but not financially aware.

That realization marked the beginning of my transformation.

## Why I Am Writing This Book

Everyone may not have a Pawan in their life. Not everyone will accidentally meet a friend who becomes a mirror.

Many people continue earning and spending for years without realizing what they are missing. I am writing this book so that you do not have to feel the guilt I felt at 30.

If you are in your twenties, start today. If you are in your thirties, start now. If you are in your forties, start seriously.

This book is not a theoretical guide.

This book provides practical ways to become financially free for people of all age groups.

It is a collection of mistakes I made—and the lessons I learned while correcting them.

Here, I will share:

- Various myths salaried people have, which bar them from becoming financially free.
- The magic of the THREE STEP FINANCIAL FREEDOM model, which no one shares.
- How to automate your investments and focus more on your office work.
- How to invest systematically instead of emotionally.
- How compounding works in your favor when given time.
- Why term insurance is essential and how to calculate the right coverage.
- How to protect your financial health before chasing returns.

- Ideal composition of your investment to achieve your financial targets.
- Worksheets to calculate Emergency Fund, Life Insurance coverage, Health Insurance coverage, Financial Goals, Investment composition, etc.
- A foolproof method to attain ₹100 crore ethically.

In one line, this book is a one-stop solution for managing your money wisely.

## A Promise to You

By the time you finish this book:

- You will not feel confused about financial products.
- You will not buy insurance blindly.
- You will not delay investing out of ignorance. You will understand how much to invest and at what stage of life. You will appreciate the power of starting early.
- You will have a systematic guide, helping you generate the wealth.
- **You will get a detailed four-week plan, which will change your life forever.**
- Most importantly, you will not regret your financial decisions.

Because financial regret is one of the most painful regrets. You can recover financial losses; you can recover lost reputation, but you cannot easily recover lost time in compounding.

## The Question You Must Answer

As you read this chapter, ask yourself: If you meet a friend five years from now, will you feel proud of your financial growth—or shocked by what you missed?

Will your money be working for you? Or will you still be working only for money? My story began with spending without thought. It changed with one conversation.

Let this book be that conversation for you.

Your salary is powerful. Your time is limited. Your future depends on what you do next.

Turn the page.

# Chapter 2

# The Seven Money Myths That Keep Salaried People Poor

Before starting this book, I deliberately spoke with dozens of salaried professionals across different industries. I wanted to understand how they think about investing. More importantly, I wanted to uncover what was preventing them from building long-term wealth.

During these discussions, one pattern became very clear. The problem was not a lack of income or a lack of opportunity. The problem was not even a lack of intelligence.

The problem was that many salaried professionals were being held back by a few deeply ingrained beliefs about money and investing. Beliefs that sounded logical on the surface, but deep inside, they were quietly limiting their financial growth.

I realized that a majority of salaried individuals are trapped in seven common myths about investing. These myths create hesitation, fear, and delay. They prevent people from starting early, investing confidently, and allowing compounding to work its magic.

In the next few sections, I will break these seven myths — one by one — and replace them with clarity, logic, and practical understanding.

## Myth 1: You need a high salary to become rich

Many young professionals assume that serious investing can wait until their salary becomes "big enough." The logic sounds reasonable: "First increase income, then think about wealth." But this belief is deeply misleading.

***Wealth creation does not begin when income becomes large. It begins when the habit of investing begins.***

In reality, the early years of a career are the most powerful years for wealth building. Expenses are relatively lower, responsibilities are fewer, and — most importantly — time is on your side. Yet this is precisely the phase most people waste, waiting for a higher salary that always seems just one increment away.

This is the first and one of the most expensive myths in personal finance: the belief that a high salary is required to become rich.

We reassure ourselves with comforting thoughts: "I have many years ahead to invest." "Once my salary increases, I will start saving seriously." "There is no hurry to make financial plans." "Insurance and long-term investments can wait."

This mindset feels harmless. But it silently delays wealth creation.

In The Psychology of Money, author Morgan Housel shares the remarkable story of Ronald Read — a man whose life quietly challenged the common definition of wealth. Ronald Read spent most of his working life in modest jobs, including years at a gas station and later as a janitor at some company. His career was ordinary. His lifestyle was simple. There was nothing glamorous about his income or profession.

When he passed away in 2014 at the age of 92, the revelation surprised many. Read had accumulated a net worth of more than $8 million. He bequeathed $2 million to his stepchildren and over $6 million to his local hospital and library.'

He did not build a company. He did not earn a massive salary. He simply invested consistently and patiently over the decades.

The lesson is unmistakable: wealth creation does not demand a high salary. What it truly demands is discipline, time, and steady consistency.

The belief that "I will start when I earn more" is one of the costliest financial myths. Wealth does not begin when income rises. It begins when the habit of investing begins.

Let me share another example.

*Putan Babu, now 50 years old, works as a househelp in Mumbai. He often recalls the day, at just 15, when he boarded a crowded general compartment train from Kolkata to Mumbai after his father's death. With little money and heavy responsibility, he arrived in the city of dreams and began living in a small chawl in Bhayander area, sharing space with labourers from his village.*

*Life was simple. Income was limited. Every rupee mattered.*

*When he was around 18, earning ₹650 per month, his house owner gave him an unexpected instruction: "Save ₹100 every month and invest it in this newly launched mutual fund." For a boy struggling to survive in a new city, ₹100 was not a small amount. Yet he obeyed.*

*Over the years, Putan forgot the name of the fund. But he never forgot the discipline. Month after month, without fail, he continued investing ₹100 through SIP. No market knowledge. No financial education. Just consistency.*

*Recently, he met his old house owner again. The owner casually asked, "Are you still investing in that fund?" Putan smiled and replied with humility, "How can I stop, Malik? It was your order. I am still investing ₹100 every month."*

*Curious, the house owner checked his folio. The result was astonishing. The fund, launched on January 1, 1995, had grown at a CAGR of 19%. Putan Babu's small monthly investment had quietly compounded into ₹21.73 lakh.*

No big salary. No complex strategy. Just time, discipline, and the power of compounding. A higher salary, by itself, does not create wealth. Compounding does.

***Income may increase your lifestyle, but compounding increases your net worth.*** The real engine of financial freedom is not how much you earn — it is how early and how consistently you invest.

To help you understand this more clearly, look at the table below. It shows **how much you need to invest every month, assuming a 12% annual return, to accumulate ₹1 crore by the age of 60.**

As you go through the numbers, notice one powerful factor at play — time. The goal remains the same. The return remains the same. Only the starting age changes. And that single variable dramatically alters the monthly investment required.

Study the table carefully. It may completely change the way you think about starting early.

| Your Present Age | Required Monthly Investment | Daily Saving |
|---|---|---|
| 21 | ₹959 | ₹32 |
| 25 | ₹1,555 | ₹52 |
| 30 | ₹2,861 | ₹95 |
| 40 | ₹10,109 | ₹337 |
| 45 | ₹20,017 | ₹667 |
| 50 | ₹43,471 | ₹1,449 |
| 55 | ₹1,22,444 | ₹4081 |

Look at this table once again. Then look at your age.

If you are 21, you need just ₹959 per month — barely ₹32 per day — to become a crorepati by 60 at 12% annual return. That's less than the cost of a cup of tea and a snack. But wait till you see what happens if you delay.

At 25, the required amount jumps to ₹1,555 per month. At 40, it crosses ₹10,000. And start at 50? You need

₹43,471 monthly. And if you wake up at 55, the number explodes to ₹1,22,444 per month.

The goal is the same — ₹1 crore at 60. The return is the same — 12% per year. The only thing changing is time.

This is the silent magic of compounding. In wealth creation, time amplifies results far more powerfully than the size of the investment. When you start early, your money earns returns, and those returns earn further returns. Over decades, this snowball becomes an avalanche. But when you delay, you are forced to compensate for lost time with much larger investments.

Time is the most powerful wealth-building asset you will ever own — and unlike money, it cannot be borrowed later.

**The earlier you start, the easier it gets. The later you start, the heavier it feels.**

So, even with a very small amount, by starting early, you can create a fortune.

## Myth 2: Salaried people cannot become rich

There is a deeply rooted myth in our society: "*Salaried people cannot become rich.*"

This belief is repeated so often that many employees accept it as truth. We assume that only business owners, startup founders, celebrities, or stock market experts can build serious wealth. A fixed monthly salary, we think, is meant only for survival — not for financial freedom.

But this belief is fundamentally flawed.

Let us examine it calmly.

A business owner may earn more in a good month — but income volatility is high. A salaried person, on the other hand, has something extremely powerful: *predictability*. A fixed income, credited every month, is not a limitation. It is a weapon — if used wisely.

As we read previously. Ronald Read, whose story is shared in *The Psychology of Money* by Morgan Housel, was neither a CEO nor an entrepreneur. He worked at a gas station and later as a janitor. His lifestyle was simple, his salary modest. Yet through disciplined, long-term investing, he accumulated more than $8 million. He did not build wealth through income size. He built it through time and consistency.

Even in India, thousands of ordinary salaried employees — teachers, clerks, government staff, private employees — have quietly built crores through systematic investing in mutual funds, provident funds, and equities over decades. They did not make headlines. But they made wealth.

Let us think practically.

A salaried professional earning ₹50,000 per month who invests 20% consistently and increases investments with every increment can build substantial wealth over 25–30 years. With the power of compounding, small disciplined investments grow exponentially.

Wealth creation does not demand irregular windfalls. It demands regular discipline.

In fact, salaried people may have an advantage:

- Regular income
- Automatic investment through SIPs
- EPF and retirement benefits
- Structured increments
- Lower temptation of risky speculation

The real barrier is not salary. It is behavior.

Most salaried individuals increase their lifestyle faster than their investments. When income rises, expenses rise first. If that pattern is reversed — if investments rise first — wealth becomes inevitable.

The myth survives because people confuse "high income" with "wealth." They are not the same. Wealth is what you keep and grow, not what you spend.

Financial freedom for salaried people is not a fantasy. It is a formula:

**Consistent saving + Long-term investing + Time + Patience.**

Salary is not the obstacle. Lack of discipline is. And discipline is fully within your control.

## Myth 3: Fixed deposits are safer and better than equity

Another prevailing common belief among salaried professionals is this: **"Fixed Deposits are safer and therefore better than equity."**

Safety feels comforting. A guaranteed return feels peaceful. No volatility. No panic. No news headlines disturbing your sleep.

But the real question is not: What feels safe today? The real question is: What protects your future?

Let us understand this through a simple story.

Jay and Abhishek worked in the same company. Both received a bonus of ₹5 lakh in January 2007 Both decided to invest the money for their children's education, which they would need after 18 years.

Jay chooses certainty. He invests ₹5,00,000 in a bank Fixed Deposit at 7% per annum.

Abhishek chooses growth. He invests ₹1,00,000 each in five different mutual funds.

The journey is not smooth for Abhishek.

In the early years, the after-effects of the 2007 financial crisis hurt markets. There were periods of negativity. Between 2014 and 2019, markets surged strongly. Then came COVID-19. Markets crashed sharply. Abhishek and his wife were upset seeing the portfolio fall. Jay, meanwhile, was relaxed. His FD quietly compounded every year without drama.

But markets do not move in straight lines — they move in cycles.

After COVID-19, markets rebounded sharply. Over 18 years, despite multiple crashes and volatility, Abhishek's portfolio delivered an average CAGR of 13%.

In 2025, both went to withdraw their investments.

Jay received ₹16,89,966.

Abhishek received ₹45,12,133.

What!!!!!!

The difference between 7% and 13% does not look dramatic on paper. It is just 6 percentage points. But compounding does not work in percentages — it works in magnitudes.

Even a 1% difference over long periods creates a significant gap. A 6% difference over 18 years creates a wealth explosion.

Fixed Deposits give stability. Equity gives growth.

The real risk is not volatility. The real risk is earning too little to beat inflation and achieve your goals.

For long-term goals, growth matters more than comfort. And compounding rewards those who allow time to work through temporary storms.

Let's see the table below and observe what creates the real magic:

| One time invested ₹5,00,000 | | |
|---|---|---|
| **Rate of Growth** | **Years of Investment** | **Final Amount** |
| 5% | 30 Years | ₹21,60,971 |
| 6% | 30 Years | ₹28,71,746 |
| 7% | 30 years | ₹38,06,128 |
| 8% | 30 Years | ₹50,31,328 |

At first glance, a 1% difference in return appears insignificant. It feels too small to matter. Many investors negotiate hard for a 0.5% discount while casually accepting a 1% lower return on their investments — without realizing what that actually costs them.

Look at the table above. A one-time investment of ₹5 lakh for 30 years at 5% grows to ₹21 lakh.

Increase the return by just 1% to 6%, and the same ₹5 lakh becomes ₹28 lakh.

That small 1% increase creates an additional ₹7 lakh. Now move from 5% to 7%. Just a 2% jump. The final amount becomes ₹38 lakh.

Pause and absorb this.

From 5% to 8% — only a 3% difference — the final wealth is almost ₹29 lakh higher.

Nothing changed except the rate of return. The time period remained the same. The investment amount remained the same.

Each extra 1% does not simply add more money — it multiplies the growth curve. Over long periods like 20 or 30 years, small differences in return create massive differences in outcome.

This is why choosing the right asset allocation matters. This is why long-term equity exposure matters. This is why settling for "safe but low" returns can quietly cost you lakhs.

When you invest for decades, you are not just investing money. You are investing time. And time magnifies every percentage point.

In wealth creation, 1% is never "just 1%." It is the difference between average and extraordinary.

## Myth 4: The Stock Market is Gambling

Another powerful myth that prevents salaried professionals from building wealth is this: **"The stock market is gambling."**

We often hear statements like — "The stock market is pure speculation." "You can lose everything." "Your money can become zero overnight."

At first, these fears appear reasonable. After all, markets fluctuate. Prices rise and fall every day. News headlines amplify panic. Stories of losses spread faster than stories of disciplined wealth creation.

But this is a half-cooked truth.

The stock market becomes gambling when it is treated like a casino. When someone trades daily based on tips, speculates in futures and options without understanding risk, or chases quick profits — that behaviour resembles gambling. Short-term speculation driven by greed and fear is not investing.

However, long-term investing is fundamentally different.

When a salaried person invests consistently in well-managed mutual funds or fundamentally strong companies for 15–20 years, they are not gambling. They are participating in the growth of businesses, industries, and the economy itself.

History provides powerful evidence.

The United States stock market has witnessed some of the worst financial crises in modern history — the Great

Depression of 1929, Black Monday in 1987, the Dotcom Bubble of 2000, the 2008 Global Financial Crisis, and the COVID-19 crash. Each time, fear dominated headlines. Each time, people predicted the end of markets.

Yet over the long term, the Dow Jones Industrial Average has delivered a CAGR of above 10%.

Similarly, the Bombay Stock Exchange, despite economic slowdowns, political changes, scams, global crises, and pandemics, has delivered a CAGR of above 14% since inception.

Markets fall. But economies grow. Businesses innovate. Productivity increases. And over long periods, markets reflect that growth.

**Gambling is driven by chance; long-term investing is driven by patience and time.**

For a salaried professional with discipline, patience, and a long horizon, the stock market is not a casino. It is one of the most powerful wealth-creation tools available.

The real risk is not market volatility, but staying away from growth for too long.

## Myth 5: Health Insurance is for older people or Heath Insurance is very Expensive

Another dangerous myth among salaried professionals is this: "**Health insurance is for old people.**" Or, "**Why should I pay thousands every year when I am perfectly healthy?**"

When we are young and fit, hospitalization feels distant. We focus on saving, investing, planning for our child's education and retirement. Insurance feels like an unnecessary expense. We tell ourselves, "*I will buy it later, when I grow older.*"

This is one of the costliest assumptions a middle-class family can make.

Health insurance is not purchased because you are ill — it is purchased while you are still healthy enough to qualify easily and affordably.

Let me explain through a simple story.

Ravi and Satu were colleagues and close friends. Both were disciplined investors. Both were saving regularly in mutual funds for their children's future.

The only difference? Ravi had taken a health insurance policy for his family, paying around ₹1,000 per month. Satu believed it was unnecessary. "We are healthy," he would say. "Why waste money?"

One evening, while returning from an official trip, their car met with a serious accident. Both were critically injured and rushed to a private hospital. Surgeries were performed. ICU care was required. After two days, they regained consciousness.

Then came the hospital bill — ₹8 lakh.

Ravi informed his insurance company. The claim was processed, and the bill was settled. He focused on recovery.

Satu had no insurance.

To pay the hospital, he had to withdraw money from his mutual funds — the very corpus he had built for his daughter's college education. Years of disciplined investing were disrupted in one incident.

Both suffered the same accident. Both received the same treatment. Both survived.

But financially, their futures looked very different.

The difference was just ₹1,000 per month.

Medical emergencies do not send invitations. Treatments today easily cost ₹5–10 lakh in private hospitals. Medical inflation is rising faster than general inflation. A single hospitalisation can wipe out years of savings. In many cases, it pushes families into debt.

Health insurance is not an expense; it is protection for your dreams.

People insure their car but hesitate to insure their own health — the very source of their income.

Financial freedom is not just about growing wealth. It is also about protecting it. Investments create assets. Insurance helps us prevent those assets from being destroyed.

When you are healthy, insurance feels unnecessary or optional. When you face a hospital bill, it becomes priceless.

At the cost of a few outings every month, you can protect lakhs of savings and ensure that one unexpected incident does not derail your long-term goals.

Health insurance is not for old people. It is for responsible people who want their financial dreams to survive uncertainty.

In the coming chapters, I will reveal the magical secret which would help you save a lot of money in health insurance plans.

## Myth 6: Term insurance is a waste of money if you survive

One of the most common myths among salaried professionals is this: **"Life insurance is a waste of money."**

Many people feel that if they survive the policy term, the premium paid is "lost." Since there is no maturity value in a pure term plan, they assume there is no benefit. As a result, they delay or completely avoid buying life insurance.

But pause for a moment and ask yourself: *What will happen to your family if your income stops tomorrow?*

Your EMIs will continue. School fees will continue. Household expenses will continue.

In India, if you even mention this at home — "What if something happens to me?" — the immediate response is emotional: "Don't say such things." We avoid discussing death because it is uncomfortable. But ignoring a reality does not remove it.

The truth is simple: death is certain, timing is uncertain. Financial responsibility begins with accepting this fact.

If you are the earning member of your family, your income is the foundation of their lifestyle. Your children's education, your home loan repayment, your retirement planning — everything depends on your earnings. If that income suddenly disappears, what replaces it?

You may have investment goals and a growing portfolio. But without adequate life insurance, those goals are vulnerable. Investments build wealth slowly over time. Life insurance provides immediate protection.

And here is the surprising part.

A healthy 25-year-old can buy a term insurance cover of ₹1 crore for less than ₹20 per day. That is cheaper than a Samosa. For this small daily cost, your family can receive ₹1 crore in case of your untimely death.

This is not an investment. It is protection.

Many salaried individuals make the mistake of mixing insurance with investment. They purchase policies that promise savings plus insurance, receive low returns, and later conclude that insurance is useless. But pure term insurance is designed only for one purpose — income replacement.

Think of it logically.

You insure your car. You insure your house. But the most valuable asset in your family is your earning capacity. If that is not protected, your financial plan stands on weak ground.

Life insurance is not about expecting the worst. It is about preparing for it. It ensures that if you are not there, your family can maintain their standard of living, continue children's education, and clear outstanding liabilities without financial distress.

Financial freedom is not only about wealth creation. It is also about risk management. A strong financial plan always includes both — growth and protection.

In the coming chapters, you will learn how to calculate the right insurance cover, choose the correct policy term, and avoid costly mistakes that many salaried professionals make.

For now, remember this:

For the price of a cup of tea each day, you can create a financial safety net of ₹1 crore for your family.

That is not a waste of money. That is a responsibility. That is a shield for your investment plans.

## Myth 7: I do not understand investing, I am not a commerce graduate

Another common myth that quietly holds back thousands of salaried professionals is this: **"I am not a commerce graduate. I do not understand investing."**

Many people believe that investing is only for finance experts — people who can read balance sheets, analyse annual reports, understand price-to-earnings ratios, and predict market cycles. If they come from a non-commerce background — engineering, medicine, arts, government service, or any other field — they assume wealth creation through investing is not for them.

This belief is not a limitation. It is an excuse.

Let us be honest. How many successful long-term investors actually read 200-page annual reports regularly? How many salaried professionals actively track quarterly earnings? The truth is, long-term wealth creation does not require complex financial analysis. It requires discipline, patience, and consistency.

Think back to the example of Putan Babu.

He came to Mumbai at a young age, worked as a househelp, and earned a modest income. He did not study finance. He did not understand market cycles. He probably could not explain CAGR. Yet he invested ₹100 every month in a mutual fund for years. He did not try to time the market. He did not panic during downturns. He simply stayed consistent.

Over time, compounding did the heavy lifting.

Today, investing has become even simpler. Systematic Investment Plans (SIPs) in mutual funds allow salaried individuals to invest automatically every month. You do not need to select individual stocks. You do not need to predict market highs and lows. Professional fund managers handle portfolio decisions. Your role is simply to start and to continue.

If understanding every technical detail were necessary, most wealthy investors would not exist.

The myth of "I don't understand finance" often hides a deeper truth — fear of starting. It feels safer to say, "This is not my field," than to learn the basics and take action.

You do not need to be a commerce graduate to understand three simple principles: *Spend less than you earn. Invest consistently. Give time for compounding to work.*

That is the foundation of wealth creation.

Financial freedom is not about academic qualification. It is about behaviour. An MBA in finance without discipline will not build wealth. A simple salaried employee with consistent investing habits can.

Do not let educational background become a barrier. Compounding does not check your academic background — it simply rewards those who give it enough time.

If Putan Babu could build wealth with ₹100 per month, and Ronald Read could build millions with ordinary jobs, what is stopping you?

Not knowledge.
Not qualification.
Only hesitation.

# Chapter 3

# Real Struggles of Salaried Persons

If you feel financially stuck despite earning regularly, you are not alone. Many salaried professionals experience this quiet frustration. The salary comes on time. Promotions happen gradually. Increments arrive each year. And yet, the feeling of financial stability seems slightly out of reach.

The salaried class carries invisible financial pressure every day.

From the outside, it looks secure — a steady job, predictable income, structured life. But internally, there is a constant balancing act. EMIs, school fees, rent, groceries, family expectations, rising fuel prices, social commitments — all moving together like gears in a machine that cannot stop.

Most of us wake up not just to earn, but to sustain.

We often feel that no matter how much we plan, something unexpected appears. A medical expense. A school fee hike. A sudden repair. An unavoidable social function. It is common to think, “Once my salary increases a little more, things will become easier.” Yet even after increments, the pressure remains.

This chapter is not about blaming you. It is not about pointing out what you should have done differently. It is about understanding your reality.

Because the truth is simple — the struggle you feel is common. It is not a personal failure. It is a structural challenge.

Most salaried individuals are trying to manage today’s expenses while worrying about tomorrow’s uncertainties. We want to maintain a certain lifestyle. We want to provide the best education to our children. We want dignity in retirement. We want security for our family. But we also want to live well in the present.

This tension creates stress.

**The solution to financial stress is structure, not sacrifice.**

Read that again.

You do not need extreme frugality. You do not need to stop enjoying life. You do not need to give up every comfort.

What you need is financial architecture.

Structure means designing your money flow intentionally. It means creating clarity instead of chaos.

Structure begins with an income allocation system — deciding in advance how much of your salary goes toward expenses, investments, protection, and savings. It also includes building an emergency fund — so that unexpected expenses do not disturb long-term goals.

It requires proper insurance protection — so that one medical event or income loss does not destroy years of effort.

It involves SIP automation — so investing becomes a habit, not a monthly decision. It demands goal-based investing — so money has purpose, not just accumulation.

And it requires periodic review — because life changes, and your financial plan must adapt with it. Most of us believe financial progress requires earning dramatically more. But in reality, financial clarity often matters more than financial increase.

When structure is missing, even a high salary feels insufficient.
When structure is present, even a moderate salary can create stability.

The purpose of bringing the day-to-day struggles of salaried persons before you is not to create fear, not to induce guilt. But to replace anxiety with clarity.

Because once structure replaces confusion, stress begins to reduce. And financial freedom stops feeling like a distant dream — and starts looking like a planned outcome.

Let me put the life of a salaried person in four bucks:

- Income Pressure
- Future Anxiety
- Risk Exposure
- Confusion & Paralysis

## Bucket 1: Income Pressure

Let us begin with the most common and most immediate struggle — income pressure.

Most of us have said at some point, *"My salary is just enough for expenses."*

It is common to feel that by the time the month ends, nothing sufficient remains to save. The intention to invest is there. The desire to build wealth is there. But the numbers don't seem to cooperate.

A typical salaried month often looks like this:

The salary is credited. For a brief moment, there is relief. A sense of comfort.

Then the deductions begin.

Home loan EMI.
Car loan EMI.
Credit card payment.
School fees.
Insurance premiums.
Utility bills.
Groceries.
Fuel.

By the second or third week, most of the money has already been assigned. By the end of the month, many people experience what can be called the "zero-balance feeling" — not literally zero in the bank, but emotionally zero in progress.

We often feel that inflation is running faster than our increments. Prices of food, education, healthcare, and housing seem to rise quietly each year. Even when income increases, expenses somehow adjust upward just as quickly.

This leads to another thought: "*I can't save because of EMIs.*"

EMIs create comfort today but pressure tomorrow. They allow us to enjoy assets immediately — a house, a car, a lifestyle upgrade. But they also lock a portion of future income before it even arrives. Over time, the monthly flexibility reduces.

Then comes lifestyle inflation.

As income grows, lifestyle grows alongside it. A better phone. A better car. More frequent dining out. Better vacations. None of these are wrong. In fact, they are often rewards for hard work. But gradually, what was once a luxury becomes a necessity. The baseline shifts upward.

We often don't notice when "optional" becomes "essential."

Social pressure adds another invisible layer.

It is common to think, "What will people say if we don't host properly?" "What will relatives think if we don't upgrade?".

In a connected world, comparison is constant. Social media amplifies it, we want to live the life, we see on social media reels. Appearances start influencing spending decisions. Not because we are careless — but because we are human.

Let us pause here and say something important:

**This is not irresponsibility. This is structure failure.**

Most salaried individuals are not struggling because they lack discipline. They are struggling because their income flows without a deliberate design. Money arrives, and expenses claim it automatically.

The problem is not necessarily low income. The problem is lack of financial structure.

When there is no predefined allocation system, spending expands to fill income. EMIs consume flexibility. Lifestyle adjusts upward. Savings get postponed.

Most of us assume that once income increases significantly, the pressure will reduce. But without structure, higher income often brings proportionately higher expenses — and the stress remains.

Income pressure is real. But it is manageable.

Not by cutting joy from life. Not by extreme sacrifice. But by designing a clear structure that tells your money where to go before others decide for it.

That shift — from reactive spending to intentional allocation — is where relief begins. You will learn how to do that in the coming chapters.

## Bucket 2: Future Anxiety: The Fear We Rarely Speak About

There is a silent anxiety that lives in almost every salaried professional's mind. It may not be discussed openly at dinner tables, but it shows up in quiet moments — late at night, during school fee payments, or while reading news about rising prices.

**"Inflation is rising."**
**"Education costs are increasing every year."**
**"Will I have to work even after retirement?"**

These are not irrational fears. They are real.

Look at education costs today. A good private school education already costs several lakhs over the years. A professional degree from a reputed college can cost ₹15–25 lakh or more. Now imagine what that number might look like 15 years from today. Even if costs simply double — which is not unrealistic — are we preparing for that reality?

Pause and ask yourself gently:

If your child dreams of becoming a doctor, engineer, designer, or studying abroad —

**Will finances support that dream, or limit it?** Will your child choose a career based on passion — or affordability?

That question carries emotional weight.

Now think about retirement.

Most salaried individuals are so busy managing current expenses that retirement feels distant. But time moves quietly. One day, salary credits will stop. Monthly income will not arrive automatically. Yet expenses will continue — groceries, medical costs, utilities, social responsibilities.

If your current monthly expense is ₹50,000, what will it be 20–25 years later? Even at modest inflation, it could easily become ₹1 lakh or more. Have you built a corpus that can generate income for 25–30 years after retirement?

Or will you depend on children? Or continue working out of necessity, not choice?

There is nothing wrong with working after retirement — if it is by passion. But working because you cannot afford to stop creates a different kind of pressure.

This future anxiety often creates two reactions: worry or avoidance. Some constantly worry but do not act. Others avoid thinking about it altogether.

But here is the comforting truth: **future anxiety reduces when there is a plan.**

Uncertainty creates fear. Structure creates clarity.

When you know:

- How much you roughly need
- How much you are investing monthly
- How long your money has to grow

The anxiety begins to soften.

Long-term planning does not eliminate challenges. But it replaces helplessness with control. The future will always be uncertain. But being unprepared is optional. You cannot stop inflation. But you can outgrow it.

And when you plan early, you are not just building wealth — you are protecting dreams, dignity, and independence.

By the time you will finish this book, you will have a clearly defined structured plan that every salaried person needs to know.

## Bucket 3: Risk Exposure: The Threat We Prefer Not to Think About

There is another fear that silently sits in the background of every salaried household — the fear of an unexpected crisis.

We plan for vacations. We plan for school admissions. We plan for festivals and purchases.

But very few plan seriously for disruption.

Many people admit, "Medical emergencies can destroy savings." Yet the thought is uncomfortable, so it is postponed. We tell ourselves, "We are healthy." Or "Nothing serious will happen." Or simply, "We will manage somehow."

But reality does not consult optimism.

A single hospitalization in a private hospital can cost ₹5–10 lakh. A surgery, ICU stay, or prolonged treatment can go even higher. Years of disciplined SIPs can disappear in one week. The education corpus you built patiently can suddenly become a hospital payment.

And if the person hospitalized is the earning member, the situation becomes **even grave**. This is an uncomfortable but important truth: Income stopping is a bigger risk than market crashing.

When markets fall, investments fluctuate temporarily. Historically, they recover. But when income stops due to illness, disability, or death, recovery is not automatic. There is no market rebound for lost earning years.

Yet many salaried professionals worry more about stock market volatility than about protecting their income.

Another common confusion appears here:

"I don't know how much insurance I should take."

This uncertainty leads to inaction. Some remain underinsured. Some avoid buying insurance altogether. Others purchase policies without understanding coverage, just to feel "secured."

But protection is not about random decisions. It is about calculated coverage. Health insurance protects savings from medical shocks. Life insurance protects income from permanent loss. These are not luxury products. They are financial shock absorbers.

Imagine building a beautiful house on weak foundations. No matter how elegant the structure looks, one strong tremor can damage it. Investments without adequate insurance protection are similar. Growth without safety creates fragility.

This is why financial planning must follow a clear order:

**Protection first. Growth later.**

Before increasing SIP amounts, ensure you have:

- Adequate health insurance
- Sufficient term life cover
- An emergency fund

Once these are in place, you can pursue growth confidently. Without them, every investment carries hidden anxiety.

Notice something important here: this is not about creating fear. It is about reducing it.

Financial freedom is not only about multiplying money. It is about building resilience. It is about ensuring that one unexpected event does not erase years of effort.

Markets will rise and fall. But your family's stability should not.

Protection may not look exciting. It does not give visible returns. But it gives something far more valuable — continuity.

And continuity is what allows compounding to work uninterrupted for decades. In the upcoming chapter I will share an insurance calculator to find your life and health insurance need.

## Bucket 4: Confusion & Paralysis: When Too Many Choices Stop Us from Starting

There is one more struggle that rarely gets acknowledged — confusion. Many salaried professionals quietly admit: "I don't know where to invest." "There are too many options." "What if I choose the wrong one?"

And this confusion does not emerge from lack of intelligence. It comes from overload.

Today, information is everywhere. Social media influencers recommend stocks. News channels debate markets daily. Friends suggest crypto; relatives talk about real estate; banks promote fixed deposits; insurance agents push policies; and mutual fund advertisements promise high returns.

Instead of clarity, you receive noise.

When choices multiply, clarity reduces. This is called ***decision fatigue***. The human brain can handle only a limited number of complex decisions before it starts postponing them. Investing, which already feels serious and risky, becomes something you delay "until you understand it better."

So you wait.

You read more articles. You watch more videos. You compare more products.

And months — sometimes years — pass without taking action.

Ironically, in trying to avoid making the wrong decision, many people end up making the worst one: not investing at all. Over-information creates paralysis. Every option seems risky. Every expert sounds confident. You fear regret. You fear loss. You fear judgment.

"What if the market falls right after I invest?" "What if I choose the wrong mutual fund?" "What if I miss a better opportunity?"

These questions are natural. They show you care about your money.

But here is something reassuring: no investor gets every decision perfect. Wealth creation does not require perfection. It requires participation.

Confusion is natural, but often curable.

Clarity does not come from consuming more random information. It comes from having a simple structure.

When you know:

- Why you are investing
- For how long you are investing
- How much risk you can tolerate
- What role each investment plays

The noise begins to fade.

You do not need 20 products. You do not need daily market predictions. You do not need to track every headline.

You need a plan that matches your goals.

In the coming chapters, I will help you build that roadmap step by step. I will simplify asset allocation. I will discuss how to select suitable investment avenues. I will explain how to align investments with goals instead of trends. I will show how much to invest, to achieve your desired future goals.

The objective is not to turn you into a market expert. It is to turn you into a confident decision-maker, a salaried person who knows three steps of financial freedom – Protect, Invest and Compound.

Now, let us move from worry to structure.

# Chapter 4

# From Reaction to Design

## *Imagine Your Financial Life Two Years from Now*

In the last three chapters, you have been looking into a mirror.

A mirror that reflected your financial habits, your struggles, your dependence on a monthly salary, and the invisible chains that keep millions trapped in the same cycle for decades.

But this chapter is different.

This chapter is not about where you are.

It is about where you can become.

What if, two years from today, money no longer controlled your decisions?

What if your salary stopped being your survival oxygen and became just one of many income streams?

What if financial stress, fear of emergencies, and the anxiety of month-end balances slowly disappeared from your life?

The upcoming chapters are not theories. They are a structure — a practical blueprint that can transform an ordinary salary-dependent person into a truly financially free individual.

And every transformation begins with a transition.

The first two years will not be easy. In fact, they may feel uncomfortable. You will have to change the way you think, spend, save, and live. A person who once handled money casually will slowly evolve into someone disciplined, intentional, and financially powerful.

At first, the change may feel painful.

But here is the beautiful part: those two years will build the foundation for the rest of your life. A foundation so strong that once it is built, your relationship with money will never remain the same again.

And one day, without even realizing it, you will stop chasing money…

and start enjoying the journey of freedom.

Now, close your eyes for a moment and imagine your financial life two years from today. Nothing dramatic has changed on the surface. You are still earning a salary. Responsibilities still exist. The economy still fluctuates. Life still demands your time and attention.

Yet something feels different.

There is less anxiety in your thoughts. You do not feel a subtle tension every time your phone notifies you about a bank transaction. You no longer avoid checking your account balance toward the end of the month. You do not feel that constant background fear of "What if something goes wrong?"

Instead, there is steadiness.

Not extravagance. Not luxury. Not overnight wealth.

Steadiness.

That is what structure creates.

Financial stability rarely arrives with noise. It builds quietly in the background. It first changes how you feel before it changes what you own. And once your emotional relationship with money shifts, everything else begins to align naturally.

Two years from now, you are not necessarily rich. But you are organised. You are protected. You are intentional. And that changes how you experience your entire financial life.

## What Begins to Change When Structure Is Applied

When you begin implementing the structure given in this book, the transformation is subtle but powerful. The first noticeable shift is internal. The first time your emergency fund crosses three months of expenses, something inside you relaxes. You realise that if an unexpected event occurs, you will not immediately fall into panic.

You may not celebrate this milestone publicly. There may be no applause. But internally, you feel stronger. You begin to understand the value of preparation.

The first-time markets decline and your SIP continues automatically, discomfort will appear. You may feel tempted to pause it. You may hear conversations about losses. But you let it continue. Months later, when recovery happens and you see growth, you understand something important — **resilience** is more powerful than **prediction**.

Gradually, spending becomes conscious rather than emotional. Earlier, purchases may have been reactions —

to stress, to comparison, to reward yourself. Now, decisions become thoughtful. The first time you say "no" to an unnecessary expense without guilt, you realise discipline does not feel restrictive. It feels mature.

At the end of the first year, when you review your portfolio calmly, you notice something different. Instead of reacting emotionally to short-term fluctuations, you observe trends. You evaluate progress. You feel like an owner of your financial system rather than a victim of circumstances.

And slowly, your identity evolves. You no longer see yourself as someone trying to "manage expenses." You see yourself as someone building stability. That shift in identity is more powerful than any numerical milestone.

## Emotional Transformation Comes Before Financial Growth

Many people assume financial transformation is about increasing numbers. In reality, the emotional transformation comes first.

Anxiety reduces before wealth increases. Confusion fades before returns compound. Fear decreases before confidence grows.

You begin to notice subtle changes in your behaviour. You are less disturbed by market headlines. You no longer feel an urgent need to match the lifestyle upgrades of colleagues. You think in terms of five or ten years instead of five or ten days.

Retirement, which once felt distant and intimidating, begins to feel like a long-term project you are actively preparing for. Your child's education no longer feels like an overwhelming burden; it feels like a goal with a structured path.

Earlier, uncertainty felt threatening. Now, uncertainty feels manageable.

This emotional grounding is the real beginning of financial freedom. When your mind feels organised, your money begins to follow.

## Let Us Acknowledge Reality: Change Will Feel Uncomfortable

It is important to say this clearly: transformation does not begin with comfort. It begins with adjustment.

When you introduce structure into your financial life, discomfort will appear. This does not mean you are doing something wrong. It means you are stepping outside old patterns.

Reducing unnecessary expenses can feel awkward because spending is not purely logical. It is often emotional. We spend to feel rewarded after a difficult week. We spend to feel included in social circles. We spend to validate progress. When you begin controlling that impulse, it may feel unfamiliar.

Starting equity investments may create anxiety. The fear of volatility is real. The fear of making a wrong choice is natural. You may check your portfolio frequently. You may question your decisions during downturns. These reactions are not signs of incompetence. They are signs of transition.

Confusion about financial products may surface. There are too many options, too many opinions, and too much information. This overload can create paralysis. But confusion is not incapability; it is simply a lack of structure.

Lifestyle adjustments may also create social discomfort. You may hesitate before upgrading your car. You may think twice before booking an expensive vacation. You may wonder how others perceive your choices. Comparison can feel uncomfortable.

But this phase is temporary. What feels strange today becomes normal tomorrow. The discomfort you experience is not sacrifice — it is recalibration.

## Small Hurdles Will Appear Along the Way

Even with structure in place, life will test your discipline. Markets will fall. They always do. Volatility is not an exception; it is a feature of long-term growth.

When markets decline, you may momentarily doubt your approach. But if your structure is strong — with emergency funds, insurance protection, and goal-based investments — temporary fluctuations will not destabilize you.

External pressures will also arise. Friends may upgrade to bigger homes. Colleagues may buy new cars. Social media may amplify the illusion that everyone else is moving faster. In those moments, comparison may tempt you.

Unexpected expenses may disrupt your monthly plan. A medical bill, a family obligation, or an unplanned repair may temporarily disturb your savings flow. Insurance premiums may initially feel heavy because they are new commitments.

Delayed gratification can also feel frustrating. Watching others spend freely while you remain disciplined may test your patience. But remember, their spending is visible. Your stability is invisible.

Every meaningful transformation includes short-term friction. The discomfort you feel now is the cost of long-term control.

## Reframing Discomfort as Investment

Financial stability feels slow in the beginning because compounding works silently. You may not see dramatic progress in the first six months. You may not feel significantly different in one year.

But every month of discipline compounds beneath the surface. Every automated SIP reduces future stress. Every insurance premium reduces vulnerability. Every controlled expense strengthens identity.

Over time, what once felt restrictive begins to feel empowering. You stop feeling deprived. You start feeling organised.

The discomfort fades. The stability remains.

When you reframe temporary friction as long-term investment, your mindset changes. Instead of asking, "Why is this hard?" you begin asking, "What is this building?"

And the answer is simple — it is building resilience.

## What Stability Truly Looks Like

Two years from now, your emergency fund exists and is maintained. Your insurance coverage is adequate and aligned with your responsibilities. Your investments run automatically without daily interference. Your expenses reflect your priorities rather than social pressure.

You still enjoy life. You still celebrate occasions. You still spend on experiences that matter to you. But you do so without guilt and without anxiety.

When unexpected events occur, you adjust calmly. When markets fluctuate, you remain steady. When peers compare lifestyles, you feel secure in your own path.

This is not extreme frugality. It is balanced structure.

You are not eliminating joy from your life. You are protecting it.

## The Deeper Shift: From Reaction to Design

Most salaried professionals operate in reaction mode. They react to expenses, react to market movements, react to social comparison, react to emergencies.

Structure shifts you from reaction to design.

When your financial life is designed intentionally, you make fewer emotional decisions. You do not chase trends. You do not panic during downturns. You do not overspend to impress.

Instead, you follow a system.

And systems reduce stress because they remove constant decision-making.

When structure exists, willpower becomes less necessary. Automation handles discipline. Planning replaces impulse. Protection reduces fear.

This is where financial maturity develops.

## Why This Chapter Matters

This chapter is not about technical strategies. It is about psychological readiness.

If you expect transformation to feel comfortable, you will quit at the first sign of friction. If you assume discipline must feel pleasant, you will abandon it when it feels inconvenient.

By understanding that discomfort is natural, temporary, and necessary, you prepare yourself for sustainable change.

Financial growth is not a straight line. There will be pauses. There will be doubts. There will be moments when progress feels slow.

But if your structure remains intact, progress becomes inevitable.

## Stability Is Built, Not Gifted

Financial freedom does not arrive suddenly. It is not delivered by a single promotion, a market rally, or a lucky opportunity.

It grows quietly.

First in habits.

Then in confidence.

Then in numbers.

Most salaried individuals do not lack earning capacity. They lack structure. And structure can be built deliberately, step by step.

In the coming chapters, we will begin constructing that structure carefully. You will learn how to allocate income intelligently, how to protect against risk properly, how to automate investments efficiently, and how to align money with goals clearly.

There will be no complexity for the sake of sophistication. Only clarity for the sake of control.

Discomfort may appear, but it will not dominate you. Volatility may occur, but it will not destabilize you. Doubt may arise, but it will not defeat you.

Because once structure is in place, financial progress becomes less about emotion and more about design.

You have already moved from ignorance to awareness. Now you are preparing to move from awareness to structured action.

Financial freedom for a salaried person is not a fantasy. It is not reserved for the extraordinary. It is not dependent on sudden wealth.

It is designed patiently.

And we are about to begin building that design — one structured step at a time.

# Chapter 5

# The 3-Step Wealth Framework for Salaried Persons

## *Wealth Is Not Complicated*

Most salaried professionals believe that wealth creation is complicated. They assume it requires advanced financial knowledge, constant market tracking, secret strategies, or access to insider advice. The world of investing appears crowded with products, advisors, jargons, predictions, and conflicting opinions. Mutual funds, stocks, bonds, insurance plans, retirement schemes, tax-saving options — everything feels overwhelming.

As discussed previously, when something feels complicated, most people delay action. And when action is delayed, compounding is delayed.

But here is the truth: wealth building is not complicated. It is sequential.

The confusion arises because people see many pieces at once without understanding the order in which those pieces fit together. Just like building a house, wealth cannot be constructed randomly. You cannot build the fifth floor before laying the foundation. You cannot install windows before the structure exists. You cannot decorate a room that has not yet been constructed.

Similarly, financial freedom is not about collecting financial products. It is about following a sequence. And the sequence is:

**Protection → Investment → Growth → Freedom**

If the order is wrong, the results suffer. Many salaried individuals try to jump directly to high-return investments without protection. Some invest aggressively without emergency savings. Others chase returns but ignore risk. The outcome is stress, inconsistency, and eventual withdrawal from the process.

Think of driving a car. You need brakes before speed. Without brakes, speed becomes dangerous. With proper brakes, you can confidently accelerate. Protection acts as the brakes in your financial journey. Once protection is in place, you can move forward without fear.

Wealth is not built by earning more; it is built by structuring what you earn.

This chapter introduces a simple, practical framework designed specifically for salaried individuals. It removes noise and replaces it with order. It is not a shortcut or a trick. It is a sequence.

And once you understand the sequence, clarity replaces confusion.

## Introducing the 3-Step Wealth Framework

The 3-Step Wealth Framework for Salaried Individuals is straightforward:

Step 1 – Protect
Step 2 – Invest Systematically
Step 3 – Multiply Through Compounding and Discipline

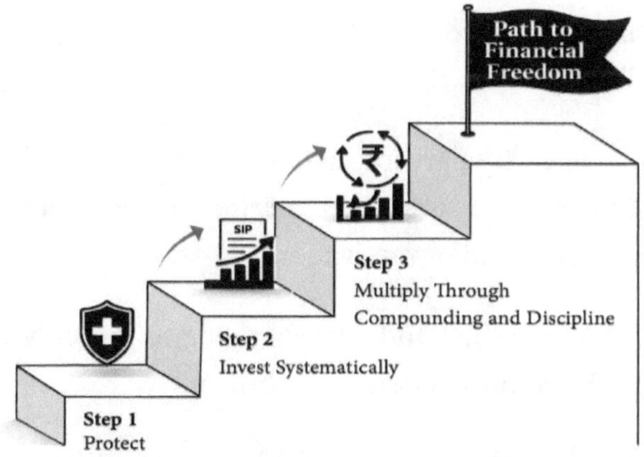

Most people attempt to start from Step 3. They want high returns immediately. They want growth without structure. They want speed without safety. But when protection is missing and systems are weak, growth becomes fragile.

This framework is not motivational advice. It is a practical roadmap.

It recognizes that salaried income is predictable but limited. It recognizes that responsibilities exist. It recognizes that risk is real. And it builds wealth in a way that respects these realities.

Let us briefly preview each step.

Step 1 ensures that your financial life cannot collapse due to one unexpected event. It protects income, health, and stability.

Step 2 converts salary into assets through automation and discipline. It ensures that wealth creation does not depend on mood or motivation.

Step 3 allows time and compounding to multiply those assets. It requires patience, not brilliance.

When these three steps are followed in order, wealth becomes inevitable over time.

Now let us examine each step carefully.

## Step 1 – Protect

Protection is the foundation. Without it, everything built on top remains vulnerable.

Life is unpredictable. A medical emergency can wipe out years of savings. An untimely death can collapse a family's financial stability. Job loss can disrupt income flow. These events are uncomfortable to discuss, but ignoring them does not reduce their probability.

Protection is not investment. Protection is a safety net.

Consider the example of Ravi and Satu. Both earned well. Both invested for their children's future. But only Ravi had health insurance. When an accident led to hospitalization, Ravi's investments remained untouched because insurance absorbed the shock. Satu, without insurance, had to liquidate investments meant for his daughter's education. One incident altered years of planning.

This is why protection comes first.

Protection has three pillars:

## 1. Term Life Insurance

If you are the primary earning member, your income supports your family's lifestyle, education, and security. Term insurance replaces that income in case of untimely death. It is not designed to give returns. It is designed to protect responsibilities.

Protection is not optional; it is foundational.

A simple term policy provides large coverage at low cost. It ensures that your financial goals survive even if you do not.

## 2. Health Insurance

Medical inflation is rising rapidly. One hospital bill can destroy ten years of disciplined saving. Employer-provided insurance may not be sufficient, especially during job transitions.

Health insurance protects your investments from being liquidated due to emergencies. It ensures that wealth-building continues uninterrupted.

You do not install CCTV after a theft. You install it before. Insurance follows the same principle.

### 3. Emergency Fund

An emergency fund covers 6–12 months of essential expenses. It protects against job loss, temporary income disruption, or unexpected obligations.

An emergency fund reduces panic decisions. Without it, even minor disturbances can force borrowing or premature withdrawal from investments.

When protection is strong, risk reduces. When risk reduces, confidence increases. And confidence allows long-term investing without fear.

Without protection, investing becomes fragile. With protection, investing becomes stable.

## Step 2 – Invest Systematically

Once protection is in place, the next step is converting salary into assets.

Salary alone does not create wealth. Investment converts income into ownership.

Most salaried individuals save whatever remains at month-end. This approach rarely works because expenses expand to consume income. The correct principle is simple: pay yourself first.

Before paying EMIs, lifestyle expenses, or discretionary spending, allocate a portion of income toward investments. This is not about extreme sacrifice. It is about priority.

Automation makes this easier.

When SIPs (Systematic Investment Plans) are automated, investments happen regardless of mood. Discipline shifts from emotional effort to structural design. You do not need to feel motivated every month. The system handles it.

Asset allocation is also important. Not all money belongs in one category. A balanced distribution across equity, debt, and other instruments reduces volatility and improves stability.

Consistency beats intensity.

It is better to invest ₹10,000 every month for 20 years than to invest ₹1 lakh occasionally and stop during volatility.

Think of salary as water. If water is poured randomly, it spreads and evaporates. But if directed through a pipeline, it reaches a reservoir.

Investment is the pipeline.

Without a pipeline, income leaks into expenses. With a pipeline, income accumulates into assets.

Increasing investments with increments accelerates growth. As salary rises, lifestyle need not rise proportionally. Directing part of every increment toward investments strengthens compounding.

Investment must be disciplined, not emotional.

This step transforms salary into a wealth-building machine.

## Step 3 – Multiply Through Compounding and Discipline

Once investments are systematic, growth begins. But growth requires time.

Compounding is the silent accelerator of wealth. It rewards patience and punishes impatience.

Earlier, we saw how even a 1% difference in return over decades creates lakhs of difference. We saw how starting early drastically reduces required monthly investment. These examples demonstrate the power of time.

Time is not just a factor. It is the multiplier.

Long-term investing means staying invested during market volatility. Markets will fall. They always do. But historically, markets recover and grow over long periods because economies grow.

The mistake most investors make is stopping during downturns. They interrupt compounding at the worst possible moment.

Wealth is built slowly, then suddenly.

In the early years, progress appears modest. Then growth accelerates as accumulated returns begin generating their own returns.

**Discipline + Time = Financial Freedom.**

Compounding rewards patience. It does not reward frequent switching, panic selling, or emotional reactions.

Step 3 is not about chasing high returns. It is about staying consistent long enough for growth to accelerate naturally.

## The Final Outcome – Freedom

When the three steps work together, something powerful begins to unfold. Protection provides stability, creating a strong foundation that shields you from unexpected shocks. Systematic investment steadily builds assets, turning disciplined effort into tangible wealth. Over time, compounding multiplies those assets, allowing growth to accelerate quietly and consistently. As assets expand, they begin to generate passive income, and passive income gradually creates freedom.

Freedom does not mean quitting your job tomorrow; it means reducing financial fear. It is freedom from constant EMI pressure, freedom from the anxiety of job insecurity, and freedom to choose work based on genuine interest rather than desperation. It is the freedom to retire with dignity and peace of mind. Financial freedom is not a single dramatic event but a steady, deliberate process. It grows quietly—first in habits, then in systems, then in assets, and finally in options. And it is these options that ultimately create true confidence.

In the upcoming chapters, we will dive deeper into each one of these steps, and see the practical aspect.

# Chapter 6

# Step One - Protect: Building the Financial Foundation

## *Growth without Protection is Fragile*

Consider a salaried professional who has been investing diligently for ten years. Through disciplined mutual fund contributions and provident fund accumulation, he has built a portfolio of ₹20 lakh. For the first time in his life, he feels financially confident. He believes he is finally moving in the right direction.

Then an unexpected medical emergency occurs. The total hospital bill amounts to ₹9 lakh. His employer-provided health insurance covers only ₹3 lakh. The remaining ₹6 lakh must be arranged immediately. With no personal health policy and no emergency fund, he is forced to redeem a significant portion of his mutual fund portfolio. Nearly one-third of ten years of patient investing disappears within days.

In another situation, the primary earning member of a family passes away unexpectedly. There is no adequate life insurance in place. The monthly home loan EMI continues. School fees remain due. Household expenses do not stop. The family, already emotionally devastated, must now confront financial instability. Long-term investments are liquidated to meet daily obligations. Carefully constructed goals collapse in the absence of protection.

In a third example, an employee loses his job during an economic slowdown. Without an emergency fund, he struggles to manage expenses. He stops his systematic investments and begins withdrawing from equity funds during a market downturn. The damage is not caused by poor investment selection, but by lack of financial cushioning.

In all three situations, the problem was not investing incorrectly. The problem was building without protection.

Investment builds wealth over time. Protection ensures that wealth is not destroyed unexpectedly. A financial plan that focuses solely on growth while ignoring risk remains structurally weak. Just as a building cannot stand securely without a strong foundation, wealth cannot survive without protection.

Before thinking about multiplying money, one must first prevent financial collapse. That is why Step 1 in the

Wealth Framework is Protect. Without this foundation, every subsequent step becomes fragile.

## Why Traditional Life Insurance Plans Are Inefficient

Many individuals purchase insurance products that combine protection with investment features, such as endowment plans, money-back policies, or Unit Linked Insurance Plans (ULIPs). These products are often marketed as "two-in-one" solutions that provide life cover along with maturity benefits.

However, combining insurance and investment typically results in inefficiency.

When you mix two distinct financial objectives—protection and wealth creation—both tend to suffer. Traditional plans often provide limited life cover relative to the premium paid, while delivering modest returns in the range of 4–6% annually. Such returns barely keep pace with inflation over long periods.

Consider the following illustration.

Suppose a 30-year-old individual seeks ₹1 crore life cover.

Under a pure term insurance plan, the annual premium may range approximately between ₹12,000 and ₹18,000, depending on health and insurer. This premium provides ₹1 crore coverage at a minimal cost.

In contrast, to secure ₹1 crore maturity benefit under a traditional endowment plan, the annual premium may exceed ₹4–5 lakh, depending on tenure and features. Over 20 years, the total premium outflow becomes substantial, and returns remain modest.

Now imagine an alternative strategy:

- Purchase a ₹1 crore term policy for ₹15,000 annually.
- Invest the remaining ₹4,85,000 annually in an equity mutual fund.

If ₹4,85,000 is invested annually for 20 years at an assumed return of 12%, the future value would be approximately ₹4 crore.

Under this approach, you receive:

- Adequate life cover through term insurance.
- Substantial wealth accumulation through disciplined investing.

This comparison highlights a fundamental principle: insurance should provide protection, and investments should generate growth. Mixing the two often reduces efficiency in both areas.

Buy insurance for protection. Invest separately for wealth creation. Since, insurance companies pay big commission on these traditional plans, agents talk about these plans only.

Then what is the solution?

## Term Insurance is True Life Insurance

Term insurance is one of the most misunderstood financial instruments, largely because it does not promise returns. It does not offer bonuses, loyalty additions, or maturity benefits. It is not designed for investment. Instead, it serves a single purpose: income replacement. Further, it does not high commission to the agents, it does not get publicity or rather push from the agents.

If you are the earning member of your household, your salary finances daily living expenses, EMIs, children's education, healthcare costs, insurance premiums, and long-term savings goals. Your income is not merely a cash flow; it is the economic engine that sustains your family's lifestyle.

Unlike physical assets such as property or gold, your earning capacity cannot be stored. It depends entirely on your continued ability to work. If that ability ceases due to death, the financial consequences extend far beyond emotional loss. The household loses the stream of future income that supports its stability.

This is where the concept of Human Life Value (HLV) becomes important. Your Human Life Value represents the present economic worth of your future earnings. If you earn ₹12 lakh annually and expect to work for another 25 years, your gross earning potential over that period is ₹3 crore (₹12 lakh × 25 years), excluding increments. That earning potential funds your family's needs and aspirations.

If this earning power disappears unexpectedly, something must replace it. Term insurance performs that function. It provides a lump-sum amount to your family in the event of your untimely death, enabling them to maintain their financial stability.

Consider the practical implications. If the primary earner is no longer present, who will service the home loan? Who will fund the children's education? Who will manage monthly household expenses? Savings alone are rarely sufficient to sustain a family for decades. Investments may exist, but they are typically built with specific goals in mind. Liquidating them prematurely disrupts long-term plans.

Term insurance addresses this vulnerability directly. It ensures that the economic value of your life is protected. Because it focuses purely on protection and excludes investment components, it remains affordable relative to the coverage it provides. This affordability makes it highly efficient.

Protection is not optional; it is foundational. A financial plan without **adequate life insurance** resembles a structure built without reinforcement. It may appear stable, but it remains vulnerable to collapse.

## How to Calculate Adequate Life Cover

Many individuals determine their life insurance coverage arbitrarily, often influenced by what an agent recommends or what feels "large enough." Such an approach can lead to severe underinsurance. A more rational method involves calculating the coverage based on income replacement and financial responsibilities. On discussion with hundreds of people, I found that majority of them have insurance coverage of less than twice their annual income.

Under coverage of insurance can derail all your financial plans. Here I will help you learn step by step, how to calculate required adequate term insurance coverage. I will tell you the concept and will also share a comprehensive calculator (worksheet) to effortlessly find the correct number.

We will use a structured Income Replacement Model.

**Life Cover Required =**

(Annual Household Expense × Years Until Retirement)

Let us apply this model step by step.

## Step 1 – Calculate Annual Household Expense

The first component involves determining the amount required annually to sustain the household's standard of living. This figure should include essential expenses and exclude discretionary personal spending that would not continue in your absence.

Essential expenses are,

- Household maintenance
- Groceries
- Utilities
- School fees
- Insurance premiums
- Loan EMIs
- Transportation
- Medical expenses

Exclude expenses that are purely personal, such as individual hobbies or discretionary luxury spending.

Assume that the monthly household expense is ₹70,000.

The annual expense therefore equals:

₹70,000 × 12 = ₹8,40,000

This means the household requires ₹8.4 lakh per year to function at its current standard.

## Step 2 – Calculate Years Until Retirement

Next, determine how many working years remain until your planned retirement age.

If the current age is 32 and the planned retirement age is 60, the remaining working years equal:

60 – 32 = 28 years

Multiply the annual household expense by the number of remaining years:

₹8,40,000 × 28 = ₹2,35,20,000

This calculation suggests that approximately ₹2.35 crore would be required to replace the income needed for essential household expenses over 28 years. While a more advanced calculation would discount for investment returns and adjust for inflation, this simplified method provides a conservative and practical estimate suitable for planning.

## Step 3 – Add Outstanding Liabilities

Any outstanding loans must be cleared to prevent financial burden on surviving family members.

Suppose:

- Home loan outstanding = ₹40 lakh
- Car loan outstanding = ₹5 lakh

Total liabilities equal ₹45 lakh.

Add this to the income replacement figure:

₹2.35 crore + ₹45 lakh = ₹2.80 crore

## Step 4 – Add Future Obligations

Next, incorporate major future expenses such as children's education.

Assume one child and estimate future education expenses at ₹30 lakh (a conservative estimate for higher education).

Add this to the previous amount:

₹2.80 crore + ₹30 lakh = ₹3.10 crore

## Step 5 – Subtract Existing Assets and Coverage

Now subtract resources already available.

Suppose:

- Current investments = ₹15 lakh
- Existing life insurance cover = ₹20 lakh

Total existing support = ₹35 lakh.

Subtract this from the total requirement:

₹3.10 crore – ₹35 lakh = ₹2.75 crore

The required life cover is therefore approximately ₹2.75 crore.

This example illustrates how significantly underinsured many salaried professionals may be. Individuals often carry life cover of ₹50 lakh or ₹1 crore, believing it to be sufficient, when their actual requirement may be more than double that amount.

## Quick Estimation Rule

For those who prefer a simplified guideline, a quick estimation method is:

Minimum Term Insurance Cover = 15 to 20 times Annual Income

If annual income equals ₹12 lakh (post tax), the minimum recommended cover ranges between:

₹12 lakh × 15 = ₹1.8 crore

₹12 lakh × 20 = ₹2.4 crore

While this shortcut is not as precise as the full calculation model, it offers a practical benchmark for salaried individuals.

## Health Insurance – The Second Pillar of Protection

If term insurance protects income from permanent loss, health insurance protects wealth from sudden erosion.

Medical inflation in India has consistently ranged between 8% and 10% annually. This means that treatments which cost ₹3 lakh a decade ago can now easily cost ₹8–10 lakh in private hospitals. Advanced surgeries, ICU stays, cancer treatments, and cardiac procedures often exceed ₹10–15 lakh in metropolitan cities.

A single hospitalization can reverse years of disciplined saving.

Unlike death, which is statistically less frequent in younger age groups, medical emergencies can occur at any stage of life. Lifestyle diseases such as diabetes, hypertension, and cardiac conditions are no longer restricted to older age groups. Accidents are unpredictable. Viral infections requiring hospitalization are common. Medical risk is universal.

Many salaried professionals assume that employer-provided group insurance is sufficient. This assumption creates vulnerability.

Employer health coverage is beneficial, but it has limitations:

- Coverage amount may be inadequate (often ₹3–5 lakh).
- Coverage ceases immediately upon job change or job loss.
- No control over policy features.
- No continuity after retirement.

Health insurance is not optional. It is an essential financial safeguard.

Buying health insurance when you are young and healthy offers three advantages:

1. Lower premium.
2. Easier medical underwriting approval.
3. Completion of waiting periods before illness occurs.

Delaying purchase increases cost and risk of exclusions. Just as you do not install fire extinguishers after a fire breaks out, you do not buy health insurance after diagnosis. Protection must precede crisis.

## Employer Policy vs Personal Policy

Let us clearly differentiate between employer-provided and personally purchased health insurance.

Employer Policy:

- Paid by employer.
- Valid only while employed.
- Coverage amount fixed by company.
- No portability control.
- Ends upon resignation or retirement.

Personal Policy:

- Owned by you.
- Independent of job.
- Portable across insurers.

- Renewable for life (as per policy terms).
- Builds no-claim continuity benefits.

Consider the following scenario.

An employee aged 42 relies entirely on employer insurance of ₹5 lakh. He resigns to switch jobs. During the gap between jobs, a medical emergency occurs. Since he does not have personal coverage, the entire bill must be paid out of pocket.

Another situation: retirement at 60. Employer insurance ceases. Purchasing a fresh policy at 60 becomes expensive and may include exclusions.

Employer insurance should be viewed as a bonus. Personal health insurance is a necessity.

If you are serious about financial stability, you must own your own policy independent of employment.

## Super Top-Up Plans – Intelligent Coverage Expansion

As medical costs rise, base coverage alone may not be sufficient. However, increasing base policy coverage significantly can raise premiums. Further, the small bills of ₹2 lakh may not impact you as hard as the bills of ₹20 lakh or more.

This is where super top-up plans become efficient.

Let us understand clearly.

Assume you purchase:

- Base health policy = ₹5 lakh.
- Super top-up policy = ₹15 lakh.
- Deductible = ₹5 lakh.

If hospital bill = ₹12 lakh:

- First ₹5 lakh paid by base policy.
- Remaining ₹7 lakh paid by super top-up.
- Total coverage available = ₹20 lakh.

If hospital bill = ₹18 lakh:

- ₹5 lakh (base policy).
- ₹13 lakh (super top-up).
- Still fully covered.

Super top-up activates only after deductible amount is crossed.

This structure is cost-effective because the probability of exceeding ₹5 lakh in a single claim is lower than smaller claims. Therefore, premiums for super top-ups are relatively very low compared to increasing base cover directly.

Super top-up is not a luxury. It is a strategic tool for affordable risk management.

## How Much Health Insurance Do You Need?

Health insurance must be determined based on age, city, family size, and financial responsibilities.

Let us create a structured model.

## Step 1 – Age-Based Minimum

Age 25–35 → Minimum ₹10 lakh base coverage.
Age 35–45 → Minimum ₹15–20 lakh coverage.
Age 45+ → Minimum ₹25 lakh coverage.

The reason coverage increases with age is simple: medical risk increases and inflation compounds over time.

## Step 2 – City Factor

Metro cities (*Mumbai, Delhi, Bengaluru, Chennai, Hyderabad, Pune*): add ₹5 lakh extra coverage because treatment costs are higher.

Tier 2 cities: Base coverage may be adequate but still consider inflation.

## Step 3 – Family Size Factor

For family floater policies:

Add ₹5 lakh for each dependent above two members.

For example: If base coverage requirement = ₹15 lakh (for couple), and you have two children, consider at least ₹20–25 lakh total.

## Step 4 – Liability and Income Factor

If you are a sole earning member, carrying home loan, or supporting aging parents,

Increase coverage by 20–30% beyond minimum.

## Quick Practical Rule

Minimum Health Cover =
(Annual Income × 1.5) OR ₹15 lakh, whichever is higher.

For example:

Annual income = ₹12 lakh.

₹12 lakh × 1.5 = ₹18 lakh.

Therefore, minimum coverage should be ₹18 lakh.

This simple rule works well for salaried professionals seeking clarity without complex calculations.

## Emergency Fund – The Silent Protector

Insurance protects against major risks. The emergency fund protects against temporary disruptions.

An emergency fund should cover 6 months of essential expenses.

If monthly expense = ₹70,000.

6 months requirement = ₹70,000 × 6 = ₹4,20,000.

This amount should be kept in highly liquid and low-risk instruments:

- Savings account.
- Liquid mutual funds.
- Short-term fixed deposits.

Emergency funds should not be invested in equity. Equity fluctuates. An emergency fund must be stable and accessible.

The purpose of emergency fund is not return generation. It is liquidity. If job loss occurs or sudden expense arises, the emergency fund prevents panic selling of investments.

It acts as a buffer between crisis and long-term assets.

## Why Protection Must Come Before Investing

Let us integrate everything.

Suppose a person begins investing aggressively in equity without:

- Adequate term insurance,
- Health coverage,
- Emergency fund.

If a market downturn coincides with a medical emergency, he is forced to sell equity at low prices to pay hospital bills. This creates double damage:

1. Loss from medical expense.
2. Loss from selling investments during downturn.

If death occurs without life cover, investments meant for long-term growth are prematurely liquidated to meet immediate needs.

Without protection, investing becomes emotionally unstable.

With protection in place:

- Health emergency is covered.
- Family income is secured.
- Temporary job loss does not force liquidation.

- Long-term compounding continues uninterrupted.

*Protection does not generate returns. Protection eliminates risk.*

And eliminating catastrophic risk is the first step toward sustainable wealth creation.

Investment without discipline is speculation. Protection enables discipline.

## The Confidence of Safety

Protection is rarely celebrated because it does not create visible wealth. However, it creates something more powerful: **Stability**.

When you know that your family is financially secure in your absence, your investing decisions become calmer. When you know that medical emergencies will not wipe out your savings, you stay invested during volatility. When you know that temporary job disruption will not destroy your financial life, you act with patience.

Protection reduces fear. Reduced fear increases discipline. Discipline enables compounding.

And compounding builds wealth.

Step 1 is not about growth. It is about strength.

In the next chapter, we will move to Step 2 - Invest Systematically. Now that the foundation is strong, we will begin constructing the wealth structure above it.

Financial freedom is not built on speed. It is built on safety first — and growth next.

I have added comprehensive calculators for Term Insurance, Health Insurance and Emergency Fund. You may use them for better understanding of your requirements.

# Term Insurance Requirement Worksheet

## Section 1 – Personal Details

| Particular | Value (Years) |
|---|---|
| Current Age (a) | |
| Planned Retirement Age (b) | |
| Yrs to Retirement (b-a) (A) | |

## Section 2 – Annual Household Expense Calculation

### i. Essential Monthly Household Expenses

| Expense Category | Monthly Amount (₹) |
|---|---|
| Household Maintenance (rent, if paying) | |
| Groceries & Essentials | |
| School / Education Fees | |
| Loan EMIs | |
| Utilities (Electricity, Internet, etc.) | |
| Insurance Premiums | |
| Transportation | |
| Medical (Routine) | |
| Other Essential Costs | |
| **Total Monthly Expense (B)** | ₹ |

### ii. Annual Household Expense

Total Monthly Expense (B) × 12

₹ ______________ × 12 = ₹ ________________

**Annual Household Expense (C) = ₹ ______________**

## Section 3 – Income Replacement Requirement

Formula: Annual Household Expense (C) × Years Remaining to Retirement (A)

₹ ________ × _____ = ₹ __________

**Income Replacement Requirement (P) = ₹ ________**

## Section 4 – Add Outstanding Liabilities

| **Liability Type** | **Outstanding Amount (₹)** |
|---|---|
| Home Loan | |
| Car Loan | |
| Personal Loan | |
| Education Loan | |
| Other Liabilities | |
| Total Liabilities | ₹ |

**Total Liabilities (Q) = ₹ __________**

## Section 5 – Add Future Financial Obligations

Estimate future education costs conservatively

| Future Goal | Required Amount (₹) |
|---|---|
| Child 1 Higher Education | |
| Child 2 Higher Education | |
| Marriage Corpus (if planned) | |
| Other Major Goals | |
| **Total Future Obligations** | ₹ |

**Total Future Obligations (R) = ₹ __________**

## Section 6 – Gross Life Cover Requirement

Add Income Replacement (P), Liabilities (Q) and Future Obligations (R), as calculated in the above tables:

| Component | Amount (₹) |
|---|---|
| Income Replacement (P) | |
| Total Liabilities (Q) | |
| Total Future Obligations (R) | |
| **Gross Requirement (P+Q+R = S)** | ₹ |

**Gross Life Cover Requirement (S) = ₹ __________**

Upto the Section 6, you have calculated your gross life cover requirement. Now, we will make the adjustments of our existing coverage.

## Section 7 – Existing Financial Resources

| **Existing Resource** | **Amount (₹)** |
|---|---|
| Current Investments (Liquid + Market-linked) | |
| Existing Life Insurance Cover | |
| Employer Term Cover | |
| Other Financial Assets Available to Family | |
| **Total Existing Resources** | ₹ |

**Total Existing Resources (T) = ₹ ____________**

## Section 8 – Final Required Term Insurance Cover

Formula: Gross Requirement (S) – Existing Resources (T)

| **Particular** | **Amount (₹)** |
|---|---|
| Gross Requirement (S) | |
| Less: Existing Resources (T) | |
| **Final Required Cover (U)** | ₹ |

**Your Required Term Insurance Sum Assured (U): ₹ ______**

**Important Note**

1. Always round upward to nearest ₹25 lakh or ₹50 lakh.

2. If the required sum assured amount (U) is less than 15 times of your annual income, then re-evaluate the assumption.

3. Do not underestimate expenses or ignore liabilities.

5. Do not assume employer cover is sufficient.

6. Review every 5 years or after major life events.

# Health Insurance Requirement Worksheet

*If you ever felt, what should be your health insurance cover, the following calculator will help you in estimating the number:*

## Step 1: Your Details

**1. Your Age:** ____________________

**2. Spouse Age (if married):** ____________________

**3. Number of Children (if any):** ____________________

**4. Total Family Members (Excluding Parents):**

____________

**5. Are your parents financially dependent on you?**

☐ Yes ☐ No

**6. City Type:**
☐ Metro
☐ State Capital
☐ Other

**7. Employer Health Cover Provided: ₹** __________Lakh

## Step 2: Base Family Requirement

**Are you below 40 years of age?**
☐ Yes ☐ No

If **Yes:**
₹5 Lakh × Number of Family Members (Excluding Parents)
₹5 × ______ = ₹ ______ Lakh

If **No:**
₹8 Lakh × Number of Family Members (Excluding Parents)
₹8 × ______ = ₹ ______ Lakh

**A. Base Family Requirement (Write the above result):**
₹ ______ Lakh

## Step 3: Add Parents' Coverage (If Dependent)

If parents are dependent: Add ₹10 Lakh
If not dependent: Add ₹0

**B. Parents' Coverage Addition:** ₹ ____Lakh

**C. Total (A + B):** ₹ ____Lakh

## Step 4: City Adjustment

Select only one:

☐ **Metro:** 1.2 × C
1.2 × ______ = ₹ ______ Lakh

☐ **State Capital:** 1.1 × C
1.1 × ______ = ₹ ______ Lakh

☐ **Other Cities:** 1.0 × C
1.0 × ______ = ₹ ______ Lakh

**D. Adjusted Total:** ₹ __________________ Lakh

## Step 5: Medical Inflation Buffer

Multiply D by 1.5

**Formula:**
D × 1.5 = Final Required Health Coverage

______ × 1.5 = ₹ ______ Lakh

**E. Your Ideal Total Protection Amount:** ₹ _______ Lakh

## Step 6: Adjust For Employer Cover

**F. Employer Health Cover:** ₹ _________________ Lakh

## Final Recommendation

Take a Family Floater structured **Super Top-Up Health Insurance Plan** of:

₹ ______ Lakh (E), with a deductible amount of ₹__________Lakh(F)*

*(*Note: Even your employer health insurance cover is higher keep the deductible maximum upto ₹5 lakh)*

## Why Super Top-Up?

- Much cheaper premium.
- Provides large coverage.
- Activates after deductible (deductible amount).
- Ideal for salaried employees.
- Protects long-term wealth creation.

# Emergency Fund Requirement Worksheet

## Step 1: Calculate Your Monthly Expenses

### A. Fixed Monthly Expenses

| Expense Head | Monthly Amount (₹) |
|---|---|
| House Rent / EMI | |
| Groceries | |
| Electricity / Utilities | |
| School Fees | |
| Insurance Premiums | |
| Investments (mandatory only) | |
| Transport / Fuel | |
| Other Fixed Expenses | |

**Total Fixed Monthly Expenses (A): ₹ __________**

### B. Convert Non-Monthly Expenses into Monthly Amount

If you have quarterly, half-yearly, or yearly expenses, convert them into monthly values.

| Expense | Frequency | Formula | Monthly Equivalent (₹) |
|---|---|---|---|
| | Quarterly | ÷ 3 | |
| | Half-Yrly | ÷ 6 | |
| | Yearly | ÷ 12 | |
| | Yearly | ÷ 12 | |

**Total Converted Monthly Amount (B): ₹ __________**

## Step 2: Total Monthly Expense

**Total Monthly Expense (A + B) = ₹ __________**

(This is your monthly survival number.)

## Step 3: Calculate Base Emergency Fund

Emergency Fund Rule: **6 × Total Monthly Expenses**

₹ __________ × 6 = ₹ __________

**C. Base Emergency Fund = ₹ __________**

## Step 4: Add Inflation & Safety Buffer

Multiply C by 1.25

Formula: C × 1.25 = Required Emergency Fund

₹ __________ × 1.25 = ₹ __________

## Your Required Emergency Fund ₹ _____

Notes:

# Chapter 7

# Step Two - Invest Systematically: Turning Salary into a Wealth Machine

## *Why Most Salaried People Fail at Investing*

Most salaried professionals do not fail because they lack income. They fail because they lack a system.

Observe typical investing behavior. In one month, after receiving a bonus or feeling optimistic about markets, a person may invest 30–40% of their income. The next month, due to an unexpected expense or emotional hesitation, they invest nothing. When markets rise sharply, enthusiasm increases and additional investments are made. When markets fall, fear takes over and contributions are paused.

This pattern is emotional investing.

The problem is not the intent. The problem is inconsistency.

Wealth is built through repetition, not intensity. It is not built through occasional large contributions but through disciplined, uninterrupted investing over long periods.

Many salaried individuals approach investing as a decision they must make every month. Should I invest this month? How much should I invest? Is the market too high? Is it too low? Should I wait? This repeated decision-making creates fatigue. Eventually, fatigue leads to inaction.

Investment must not remain a monthly decision. It must become a discipline.

The core shift required is simple but powerful:

Use this: **Income – Savings = Expense**
Not this: **Income – Expense = Savings**

When you wait to see what remains at the end of the month, nothing meaningful remains. Expenses expand to match income. Lifestyle quietly absorbs increments. Social expectations increase. Comfort grows.

Systematic investing begins when savings become the first obligation, not the last adjustment.

In previous chapter, you built protection. Now, in Step 2, you build the mechanism that converts salary into assets.

Your salary must stop being consumption fuel. It must become wealth fuel.

## The "Pay Yourself First" Principle

The "Pay Yourself First" principle is not motivational language. It is operational strategy.

When salary is credited into your account, that moment determines your financial future. If the entire salary remains in your primary account, it psychologically becomes available for spending. Every expense feels justified because the money is visible.

The key is to remove visibility.

If your salary is credited on the last working day of the month, set an automatic transfer instruction dated the 2nd of the following month. That transfer should move your predetermined investment percentage into a separate investment account. The gap of one or two days ensures salary credit is settled, and the system functions smoothly.

Once this transfer happens automatically, lifestyle adjusts to the remaining balance.

This is a powerful psychological shift. When ₹20,000 is automatically moved out of a ₹1,00,000 salary, your working balance becomes ₹80,000. You begin planning within ₹80,000. There is no negotiation with yourself. There is no emotional debate.

The human mind negotiates with visible money. It rarely negotiates with money that has already been moved.

Pre-deciding your investment percentage eliminates internal bargaining. Instead of asking each month "How much should I invest?", you operate under a rule: "I invest 20% of my salary."

***Rules reduce friction. Systems reduce emotion.***

Without a predefined percentage, investing becomes reactive. With a percentage, investing becomes automatic.

Your future self must be paid before your present self begins spending

# The Four-Account System Model

To operationalize systematic investing, you need structure. The simplest and most effective structure for salaried professionals is the Four-Account Model.

This model separates money by purpose, reducing confusion and eliminating accidental misuse.

### Account 1 – Income Account

This is the account where your salary is credited. It serves only as a transit account. No spending should occur directly from this account. Its purpose is temporary holding.

### Account 2 – Investment Account

On a fixed date (preferably 2nd of every month), a standing instruction transfers a predetermined percentage from the Income Account into the Investment Account. This account is used exclusively for SIPs, retirement contributions, and long-term investments.

No expenses are paid from this account.

### Account 3 – Expense Account

After the investment transfer is executed, the remaining amount in the Income Account is transferred to the Expense Account. This account handles monthly living expenses, EMIs, utilities, groceries, and discretionary spending.

Because investments are already separated, there is no confusion regarding how much is safe to spend.

### Account 4 – Emergency Fund Account

This account remains separate, preferably in a different bank, to reduce temptation. It holds six months of essential expenses and is accessed only during genuine emergencies.

### How the Flow Works

Salary → Income Account
Auto Transfer (15–25%) → Investment Account
Remaining Balance → Expense Account
Emergency Fund → Maintained Separately

This structure eliminates monthly thinking.

There is no emotional investing. There is no accidental spending of investment money. There is no ambiguity regarding how much can be spent.

When structure exists, discipline becomes effortless.

## Step-by-Step Implementation Model

Let us now make this operational.

### Step 1 – Build the Emergency Fund

Before increasing investments aggressively, ensure that your emergency fund equals at least six months of essential expenses.

If monthly essential expenses are ₹70,000:

₹70,000 × 6 = ₹4,20,000.

This amount should be accumulated gradually over 5–6 months if not already available.

Do not invest this in equity. Equity fluctuates. Emergency funds must remain stable and accessible.

The primary purpose of the emergency fund is to prevent stopping SIPs during crises.

When emergencies occur and no buffer exists, investments are interrupted. That interruption damages compounding more than market volatility.

### Step 2 – Fix Your Investment Percentage

Investment percentage should be determined by age and responsibility.

- Age 22–30: Aim for 20% of salary.
- Age 30–40: Target 25%.

- Age 40+: Move toward 30% if feasible.

These are targets, not rigid laws. However, discipline must be non-negotiable. Even if you start at 15%, the rule must remain consistent. In upcoming sections, I will give you a worksheet to calculate your investment percentage.

**The objective is to convert investing from effort to habit.**

### Step 3 – Use Standing Instructions

Never manually invest each month.

Manual investing invites emotion. If the market falls, you hesitate. If expenses increase, you postpone. If salary feels tight, you reduce.

Standing instructions eliminate emotional interference. SIP auto-debit ensures investment continues irrespective of market movement.

Automation removes fear.

### Step 4 – Increase Investment with Every Increment

Salary increments are dangerous if unmanaged. They often lead to lifestyle inflation.

If your salary increases by ₹20,000 per month, allocate at least 50% of that increment to investments.

For example:

Salary increase = ₹20,000
₹10,000 → Increase SIP
₹10,000 → Lifestyle upgrade

This rule prevents future regret.

Without this structure, expenses expand and investment percentage shrinks over time.

### Step 5 - Annual Review, Not Daily Monitoring

Many investors check portfolio values daily. This behavior increases anxiety without improving outcomes. Market movements in the short term are unpredictable. Long-term direction depends on economic growth.

Review your portfolio once a year. During review:

- Increase SIP by 10–15%.
- Rebalance asset allocation.
- Evaluate goal alignment.

Avoid constant monitoring. Wealth building requires patience, not surveillance.

## Age-Based Asset Allocation Model

Once you have arrived at the total amount you want to invest, the next important decision is asset allocation. Asset allocation determines how your investments are distributed between growth-oriented assets and stability-oriented assets. For salaried individuals, this decision must balance return potential with emotional resilience.

A simple and practical rule is the modified "Rule of 100" or "Rule of 110."

According to the Rule of 100:

**Equity Allocation (%) = 100 – Your Age**

A slightly growth-oriented version uses, which I prefer:

**Equity Allocation (%) = 110 – Your Age**

The remaining portion is allocated to debt or fixed-income instruments.

For example:

- At age 30, equity allocation would be 70–80%.
- At age 40, equity allocation would be 60–70%.
- At age 45, equity allocation would be 55–65%.
- At age 55, equity allocation would be 45–55%.

This framework provides a starting point, not an absolute prescription. Younger investors have a longer time horizon and greater ability to absorb volatility. Therefore, higher equity exposure is reasonable. As age increases, capital protection becomes increasingly important, and allocation to debt instruments rises gradually.

However, there is an important distinction between risk capacity and risk appetite. Risk appetite reflects how comfortable you feel during volatility. Risk capacity reflects your actual ability to withstand loss based on time horizon, income stability, and financial goals.

A 30-year-old with stable employment and no major liabilities has high risk capacity, even if temporary market declines feel uncomfortable. Conversely, a 55-year-old nearing retirement has lower risk capacity even if emotionally comfortable with risk.

Asset allocation should therefore be determined by time horizon first, emotions second.

The goal of allocation is not to maximize short-term returns. It is to ensure that you remain invested through all market cycles without abandoning your plan.

## Equity vs Debt Allocation Explained

To implement asset allocation correctly, you must understand the role of each asset class.

### Equity

Equity investments represent ownership in businesses. Over long periods, businesses grow as economies expand, productivity increases, and innovation drives profits. This growth translates into higher stock prices over time.

However, equity is volatile in the short term. Market declines of 10%, 20%, or even 30% can occur during economic stress. These fluctuations are normal.

Equity serves as the growth engine of your portfolio. It combats inflation and builds long-term wealth.

Equity investing does not mean, you have to invest directly in stocks, you may start investing through mutual funds.

### Debt

Debt instruments include fixed deposits, bonds, government securities, and debt mutual funds. These instruments offer relatively stable returns but limited growth potential.

Debt acts as a shock absorber. When equity markets decline, debt components stabilize the portfolio. They reduce volatility and provide liquidity for near-term needs.

A portfolio composed entirely of equity may generate higher returns during bull markets but can cause emotional stress during downturns. Conversely, a portfolio entirely in debt may feel safe but may fail to generate sufficient growth to meet long-term goals.

Balance is essential.

For salaried individuals, 100% equity is rarely advisable unless they possess exceptional risk tolerance and a very long-time horizon. A balanced allocation ensures sustainability.

Sustainability matters more than maximum return. An investor who earns slightly lower returns but remains consistent for 25 years will outperform someone who frequently changes allocation based on market emotion.

## Mutual Fund and Investment Discipline Rules

Once asset allocation is defined, discipline in execution becomes critical. Many investors sabotage their own progress through behavioral mistakes rather than poor product selection.

Below are essential discipline rules.

## 1. Direct vs Regular Mutual Funds

Mutual funds are available in two formats: Direct and Regular.

Regular plans include distributor commissions embedded in expense ratios. Direct plans eliminate these commissions and therefore have lower expense ratios.

A 1% difference in annual expense ratio may appear small, but over long periods it compounds significantly.

Consider an example:

If ₹10 lakh is invested for 20 years at 12% annual return, the future value would be approximately ₹96 lakh. However, if the return reduces to 11% due to a 1% higher expense ratio, the future value becomes approximately ₹80 lakh.

The difference of ₹16 lakh arises purely from cost. Over 25 or 30 years, this gap widens further.

If you are comfortable selecting funds independently and reviewing annually, Direct plans can improve long-term returns. If professional guidance is needed, ensure that advisory value justifies the cost.

Cost efficiency is an important element of disciplined investing.

## 2. Do Not Stop SIP During Market Falls

Market declines create fear. However, SIP (Systematic Investment Plan) works best during volatility because it enables rupee cost averaging.

When markets fall, the same SIP amount purchases more units. When markets recover, those accumulated units contribute to higher returns.

Stopping SIP during downturn interrupts this mechanism and reduces long-term gains.

Market falls are not signals to stop investing; they are opportunities to accumulate assets at lower prices.

## 3. Avoid Frequent Fund Switching

Investors often switch funds based on short-term performance rankings. A fund that tops the performance chart one year may not lead the next year. Switching frequently leads to transaction costs, tax implications, and behavioral instability.

Give a fund sufficient time—at least five years—to evaluate its performance relative to its benchmark and category.

Patience is part of discipline.

### 4. Avoid FOMO (Fear of Missing Out)

During bull markets, certain sectors or themes deliver extraordinary short-term returns. Investors rush into these segments after seeing high past returns.

This behavior typically results in buying near peaks.

Wealth is not created by chasing trends. It is built through consistent exposure to diversified equity over long periods.

Avoid jumping from fund to fund because a peer has generated higher returns recently. Long-term consistency matters more than short-term outperformance.

### 5. Avoid Tips and Noise

Television experts, social media influencers, Telegram groups, and speculative forums constantly promote quick profit ideas.

If someone could reliably generate extraordinary returns, they would not need to sell tips.

Your objective as a salaried individual is not excitement. It is steady wealth accumulation.

Noise creates distraction. Distraction creates inconsistency.

Stay focused on your allocation and automated plan.

## 6. Avoid Futures & Options and Speculative Trading

Speculative trading, particularly in derivatives such as Futures & Options, carries high risk. Even experienced professionals face significant losses.

Warren Buffett once described derivatives as "financial weapons of mass destruction." While this statement may be debated in technical circles, its warning is relevant for salaried investors.

According to a September 2024 SEBI report, "*93% of individual traders in the equity Futures and Options (F&O) segment incurred net losses*"

Your income is stable. Trading income is unstable.

Mixing stable income with speculative behavior introduces unnecessary risk. Wealth for salaried individuals is built through compounding over decades, not through short-term trading.

### 7. Never Take Loans to Invest

Leverage magnifies both gains and losses. If investments decline while loan EMIs continue, financial stress increases rapidly.

Salaried professionals, whose income is finite and fixed, cannot afford catastrophic leverage-induced losses. Invest only surplus capital, and not borrowed money.

# The Salary-to-Wealth Conversion Model

### The 4P Model for Salaried Investing

1. Protect
2. Pay Yourself First
3. Percentage Discipline
4. Passive Automation

When these four components operate together, investing becomes mechanical rather than emotional.

Protection ensures stability. Paying yourself first ensures priority. Percentage discipline ensures consistency. Passive automation ensures continuity.

Once these are established:

- No monthly decision is required.
- No emotional negotiation occurs.
- No panic interrupts the process.

Your system operates silently in the background.

Salary enters. Investment exits. Expenses adjust. Assets accumulate.

You focus on career growth, skill enhancement, and income expansion while your investment machine runs independently.

## Handling Salary Increments Wisely

As explained previously, one of the greatest threats to wealth accumulation is lifestyle inflation.

As salary increases, expenses often rise proportionately. A car upgrade replaces the old vehicle. Housing moves to a higher rental bracket. Dining frequency increases. Travel becomes more expensive.

Without structure, increments benefit lifestyle but not net worth.

Adopt an Increment Allocation Rule:

- 50% of increment → Investments
- 30% → Savings or goal-based allocation (like travel)
- 20% → Lifestyle upgrade

For example:

If salary increases by ₹20,000 per month:

₹10,000 → Increase SIP
₹6,000 → Allocate toward short-term goals
₹4,000 → Lifestyle improvement

This ensures visible lifestyle improvement while maintaining wealth acceleration.

Over time, this discipline compounds powerfully.

## Investment is Boring by Design

Systematic investing is intentionally uneventful.

There are no daily thrills. There are no dramatic stories. There is no constant action.

And that is precisely why it works.

Wealth building is boring because it is repetitive. It rewards consistency more than brilliance. It favors discipline over intelligence. It favors patience over prediction.

Your goal is not excitement. Your goal is freedom.

When investment becomes automatic, you stop thinking about markets every week. You stop reacting to headlines. You stop questioning each fluctuation.

Instead, you focus on what you control: increasing income, improving skills, enhancing career stability.

Investing becomes background machinery. Career growth becomes foreground activity.

A well-designed investment system is like an aircraft engine on autopilot. The pilot does not manually adjust the engine every minute. The system maintains altitude while the pilot focuses on navigation.

Your career is navigation. Your automated investments are the engine. If you constantly interfere with the engine out of fear or excitement, turbulence increases.

Stability comes from trusting the system.

And over time, this quiet discipline converts salary into assets, and assets into options.

In the next chapter, we will explore Step 3 — how compounding transforms disciplined investing into financial independence.

For now, your task is simple:

Fix your percentage.
Set your automation.
Define your allocation.
And remove emotion from the process.

Once this is done, you no longer invest monthly. Your system invests for you. You may refer to the worksheets given hereafter to get your numbers.

# Monthly Income & Investment Composition Worksheet

## Step 1: Calculate Total Monthly Cash Inflow

Fill all sources of income:

| Source of Income | Monthly Amount (₹) |
| --- | --- |
| Salary (Net Take Home) | |
| Rental Income | |
| Interest Income | |
| Dividend **Income** | |
| Business / Side Income | |
| Other Income | |

**A = Total Monthly Cash Inflow = ₹ __________**

This is your **Money Entry Point.**

## Step 2: Apply The 50–20–30 Rule

**Divide A (Total Monthly Cash Inflow) into Three Parts:**

| **Necessary Expenses (Max 50%)** | **Wants (Max 20%)** | **Investments (Min 30%)** |
|---|---|---|
| B = A × 0.50 | C = A × 0.20 | D = A × 0.30 |
| ₹ | ₹ | ₹ |

## Step 3: Asset Allocation Based on Age

Enter Your Age: = ______

### Equity Percentage Formula:

**E = 110 – Age.**

E = ______ %

This percentage of D will go into Equity (see last column of above table).

## Step 4: Calculate Equity & Fixed Allocation

### Equity Allocation

**F = D × (E ÷ 100) = ₹__________**

**Fixed Return Allocation:** G = D – F = ₹__________

## Equity Breakup (Total Must Equal F)

| Equity Instrument | Monthly Amount (₹) |
|---|---|
| Direct Shares | |
| Equity Mutual Funds | |
| Index Funds / ETFs | |
| Other Equity | |

**Total Equity = ₹ __________ (Must equal F)**

## Fixed Return (Total Must Equal G)

| Fixed Instrument | Monthly Amount (₹) |
|---|---|
| PPF | |
| Sukanya Samriddhi Yojana | |
| Debt Mutual Funds | |
| Fixed Deposits | |
| Other Instruments | |

**Total Fixed Return = ₹ __________ (Must equal G)**

# Goal Planning & Investment Worksheet

## Step 1: Define Your Goal

**1. Goal Name:** ____________________________
(Example: Child Education / House / Retirement / Car etc. )

**2. Required Amount Today (A) (₹):** ___________________

**3. Time to Achieve the Goal (B) (Years):** ____________

## Step 2: Adjust Your Goal for Inflation

Money loses value every year. What costs ₹10 lakh today will cost more in future.

### Use This Simple Formula:

Future Goal Amount = Present Amount × $(1+\text{Inflation Rate})^{\text{Years}}$

$$= A \times (1+\text{inflation rate})^{B}$$

For example: If inflation is 7%:

Future Value = Present Amount × $(1.07)^{\text{Years}}$

For simplicity, assume:
- Education Inflation = 7%
- General Goals = 6%
- Medical Goals = 7%

**Now Calculate Yours:**

Inflation Assumed: ______ %

Future Goal Amount = ₹ ______ × (1 + ____ )–$^{years.}$ = ₹ ________

This is the amount you will need in future for your goal.

## Step 3: Enter Expected Return from Investment

What return do you expect?

- Conservative (Debt / Hybrid): 6–8%
- Balanced Portfolio: 9–10%
- Equity Mutual Funds (Long Term): 11–13%

Expected Annual Return: ______ %

Convert this into monthly rate:

Monthly Return = Annual Return ÷ 12

Example:
12% ÷ 12 = 1% per month

Monthly Return (r) = ______ %

## Step 4: Calculate Monthly Investment (SIP)

Now we calculate how much you must invest every month.

### Simple SIP Formula:

Monthly Investment =

Goal Amount ÷
$\{[(1 + r)^{(n-1)}] \div r\}$

Where:

r = Monthly Return (in decimal form)
n = Total Months (Years × 12)

### Break It Down Step-by-Step

1. Convert years into months:
   n = Years × 12 = ______
2. Convert return into decimal:
   If 1% per month → r = 0.01
3. Apply Formula:

Monthly SIP =

Goal Amount ÷
$\{[(1 + r)^{(n-1)}] \div r\}$ = ₹ ________________

## Your Required Monthly Investment

₹ __________ per month

This is your commitment number, you need to invest this much per month to achieve your goal.

## Complete Example

Goal: Child Education
Required Today: ₹20,00,000
Time: 10 Years
Inflation: 8%

Step 1: Inflation Adjustment

₹20,00,000 × $(1.08)^{10}$
= ₹43,18,000 approx

Step 2: Expected Return = 12%
Monthly Return = 1% = 0.01

Step 3: n = 10 × 12 = 120 months

Step 4:

Monthly SIP =

43,18,000 ÷
$\{[(1.01)^{(120 - 1)}] \div 0.01\}$

= ₹19,000 approx per month

# Inflation Adjusted Value Worksheet

*(Know What Your Money Must Become)*

Inflation silently reduces the purchasing power of your money. This worksheet will help you calculate how much your current amount must grow to maintain the same value in future.

## Step 1: Enter Your Goal Details

A. Current Value of Amount (₹): ____________________

B. After How Many Years Do You Need This Amount?
____________________ Years

C. Expected Inflation Rate (% per year): ________%

## STEP 2: CONVERT INFLATION INTO DECIMAL

To use the formula, convert inflation into decimal form.

**D = C ÷ 100**

Example:
If C = 7% → D = 0.07

**Your D Value:** ____________________

## STEP 3: CALCULATE INFLATION ADJUSTED VALUE

Use the formula below.

### Formula

**$E = A \times (1 + D)^{B}$**

E = ₹ ______ × (1 + …….)$^{\cdots\cdots}$

E = ₹____________

Where:

- A = Current Value
- B = Number of Years
- C = Inflation Rate
- D = Inflation in Decimal
- E = Future Required Amount

### Your Calculation

**E = ₹ __________________**

This is the amount you must plan for in future to maintain today's purchasing power.

## Worked Example

**Goal:** Child Education

A = ₹10,00,000
B = 10 years
C = 7%

Step 1:
D = 7 ÷ 100 = 0.07

Step 2:
$E = 10,00,000 \times (1.07)^{10}$

E ≈ ₹19,67,151

Meaning: ₹10 lakh today will require about ₹19.7 lakh after 10 years.

# Chapter 8

# Step Three - Multiply Through Compounding and Discipline

## *Turning Time into Wealth: Compounding Is Slow, Then Sudden*

If you plant a mango tree today, nothing dramatic happens tomorrow. For months, it appears unchanged. In the first few years, growth is modest. The tree demands water, sunlight, and patience. There is no visible reward. But if you continue nurturing it, one day the tree matures, branches spread widely, and fruit begins to appear regularly. The years of silent growth suddenly seem meaningful.

Compounding works in the same way.

*If you read this chapter carefully and implement the ideas given here, you will become a massive wealth creating machine. To reinforce the concept, I will give ample examples.*

Compounding means earning returns not only on your original investment but also on the returns generated in previous years. Interest earns interest. Growth multiplies growth. Time becomes an active contributor.

However, this multiplication accelerates only after a base is built.

In the first 5–7 years, the majority of portfolio growth comes from your contributions. In the later years, most of the growth comes from accumulated returns.

This is why compounding feels slow in the beginning and powerful in the end.

Most people lose hope and quit before the acceleration begins. Those who remain patient ultimately build wealth.

Most people withdraw during volatility. They stop SIPs during downturns. They shift strategies after two years. They interrupt the process repeatedly. As a result, they never experience the exponential phase.

In finance, clarity brings confidence. One of the simplest tools to understand the power of compounding is the Rule of 72. It gives you a quick way to estimate how long your money will take to double, or what rate of return you need to double it within a specific time.

In this chapter, I will share the concept of compounding from various angles, to make it a part of your life.

If you want to calculate how many years it will take for your money to double at a certain rate of interest, use the formula:

$$\textbf{Time required to double (years)} = \frac{\textbf{72}}{\textbf{Rate of Interest}}$$

For example, if your investment grows at 8% per year, then your money will approximately double in 9 years (72/8).

Similarly, if you want to know what rate of return is required to double your money within a certain number of years, you can rearrange the same principle:

$$\textbf{Required rate of Interest} = \frac{\textbf{72}}{\textbf{Number of years}}$$

For example, if you want your money to double in 6 years, then you would need an annual return of approximately 12% (72/6).

This simple rule does not replace detailed financial planning, but it builds awareness. It helps you think in terms of time, growth, and discipline. Small differences in return can create large differences in outcome. And when you begin to see how time and rate work together, you begin to understand how wealth quietly multiplies.

See the below given formula:

**Future Value = Present Value $(1+r)^t$**

**(Where; r is rate of return or interest rate and t is the time period)**

If you observe the formula carefully, you will notice that the future value is directly influenced by two variables: the rate of return (r) and time (t). As these two factors increase, the future value rises significantly.

If the formula feels overwhelming, do not worry. I will explain it through multiple practical examples so that the concept becomes clear and firmly understood.

Let's see a magic of compounding in real life:

*Harish Chaudhary is just 30 years old as on December 31, 2025. He makes a single decision—and invests ₹5 lakh for his retirement on Jan 01, 2026. And then... he does absolutely nothing. No SIP. No annual top-up. Not even one extra rupee invested again.*

*Now here comes the part that will shock you.*

*If that ₹5 lakh grows at 12% per year and simply remains untouched, by the time Harish turns 60 on December 31,*

*2055, that one investment will explode to approximately ₹1.49 crore.*

**Yes, you read that correctly, he did not add any single paisa!!!!!**

₹5 lakh becomes nearly ₹1.5 crore.

| Year | Total Years | Total Value |
|---|---|---|
| Jan, 2026 | 0 | ₹5Lakh |
| Jan, 2032 | 6 | ₹9.86 Lakh |
| Jan, 2038 | 12 | ₹19.47 Lakh |
| Jan, 2044 | 18 | ₹38.45 Lakh |
| Jan, 2050 | 24 | ₹75.89 Lakh |
| Jan, 2056 | 30 | ₹1.50 Crore |

No trading.
No market timing.
No complicated strategies.

Just time and compounding.

What feels like an ordinary amount today multiplies almost 30 times over three decades. This is not luck. This is not fantasy. This is the ruthless mathematics of compounding.

When money is given time, it transforms from savings into a wealth-creating machine.

If you felt, this was magic, then let me bring a bigger magic for you

**Now prepare yourself for something even more astonishing.** If you implement this in your life, you will never be same again.

What if Harish does not stop at just one investment? What if he invests ₹5 lakh at the **beginning of every year for the next 30 years** and simply allows the money to grow at 12% annually?

Can you imagine the retirement corpus?

Any idea!!!!

Think!!!!

It would grow to approximately **₹13.51 crore**.

Yes, ₹13.51 crore.

| Year | Total Years | Money |
|---|---|---|
| **2026** | 0 | ₹5 Lakh |
| **2032** | 6 | ₹45 Lakh |
| **2038** | 12 | ₹1.35 Crore |
| **2044** | 18 | ₹3.13 Crore |
| **2050** | 24 | ₹6.62 Crore |
| **2056** | 30 | ₹13.51 Crore |

Not through business ownership.
Not through speculation.
Not through extraordinary income.

Just consistent investing combined with time.

Those who understood it built substantial wealth, while those who ignored it paid a heavy price. Compounding does not need miracles; it only needs discipline.

A simple principle governs long-term wealth creation:

You do not need extraordinary returns. You need uninterrupted compounding.

*"Compound interest is the eighth wonder of the world. He who understands it, earns it...he who doesn't......pays it."*- ***Albert Einstein.***

## Early investing vs late investing

To understand the power of time, let us examine two structured examples.

### Rahul vs Bhagat

Rahul begins investing at the age of 25. He invests ₹10,000 per month in an equity mutual fund earning an assumed average return of 12% annually. He continues this investment for 10 years and stops at the age of 35. His total contribution during this period equals:

₹10,000 × 12 × 10 = ₹12,00,000.

After the age of 35, he makes no further contributions but leaves the accumulated amount invested until age 60.

Bhagat, on the other hand, starts at the age of 35. He also invests ₹10,000 per month at 12% annual return. However, he continues investing every month until he reaches the age of 60, a total of 25 years.

His total contribution equals:

₹10,000 × 12 × 25 = ₹30,00,000.

At first glance, Bhagat appears more disciplined. He invested for 25 years compared to Rahul's 10 years. He contributed ₹30 lakh compared to Rahul's ₹12 lakh.

*(Note: Rahul invested for 10 years, whereas Bhagat invested for 25 years)*

Now let us calculate outcomes.

## Rahul's Investment

₹10,000 monthly SIP at 12% annual return for 10 years results in approximately ₹23 lakh at age 35.

If this ₹23 lakh remains invested at 12% annually for the next 25 years (from age 35 to 60), it grows to:

Future Value = ₹23 lakh × $(1.12)^{25}$

**= ₹3.91 crore**

So, Rahul ends up with approximately ₹3.91 crore at the age of 60.

## Bhagat's Investment

₹10,000 monthly SIP by Bhagat at 12% annual return for 25 years results in approximately ₹1.91 crore.

So despite investing ₹30 lakh and also for 25 years, Bhagat ends up with around ₹1.91 crore at the age of 60.

Rahul, who invested only ₹12 lakh, ends up with almost double Bhagat's corpus.

**The only difference was the 10-year head start.**

Time mattered more than amount.

This example is not theoretical exaggeration. It is the mathematical reality of compounding.

## The ₹5,000 SIP Case

Let us examine a smaller example to reinforce the idea.

**Case A:** Start at age 25
Monthly SIP = ₹5,000
Return = 12%
Duration = 35 years

Future Value (Maturity Amount) ≈ ₹3.2 crore

Total investment = ₹5,000 × 12 × 35 = ₹21 lakh

Corpus ≈ ₹3+ crore

**Case B:** Start at age 35
Monthly SIP = ₹5,000
Return = 12%
Duration = 25 years

Future Value (Maturity Amount) ≈ ₹85–90 lakh

Total investment = ₹5,000 × 12 × 25 = ₹15 lakh

Difference in starting age: 10 years.
Difference in final corpus: More than ₹2 crore.

**The contribution difference between the two investors is only ₹6 lakh. But the corpus difference exceeds ₹2 crore.**

This is compounding.

The earlier years carry disproportionate importance because they allow returns to multiply over longer periods.

You do not need a large starting amount. You need time.

So, your parties, expensive gadgets, foreign trip, new cars at the initial years of your job, may cost you a fortune.

**Moral:** Invest in early years of your service, push expenses for the later part and generate massive wealth.

## The Power of Long-Term Equity

Equity has historically delivered superior long-term returns compared to fixed-income instruments because it represents ownership in growing businesses. While returns are not guaranteed year by year, over long periods of 20–25 years, equity markets tend to reflect economic growth.

Consider an example.

Vir Singh, an MBA graduate, knows the power of interest rate, hence, invests in an SIP of ₹20,000 per month for 25 years, at **12% annual return**:

*At the end of 25th year Vir will get a maturity amount of ≈ ₹3.8 crore.*

Total Contribution Vir made = ₹20,000 × 12 × 25 = ₹60 lakh

Harry, a cricketer, on the other hand is a conservative investor, opens a recurring FD in a bank, which gives a **return of 6%.**

Similar to Vir, Harry also deposits ₹20,000 per month in his FD account for 25 years:

*At the end of 25th year Harry will get a maturity amount of appx. ₹1.4 crore from the bank.*

**Both invested same amount for the same duration, yet Vir got ₹3.8 crore, whereas Harry got only ₹1.4 crore.**

Difference is ₹3.8–₹1.4 crore = ₹2.4 crore. The difference between 6% and 12% appears small in percentage terms. But compounding magnifies this gap significantly over long durations.

However, one must also consider inflation.

If inflation averages 6% annually, a 6% FD generates zero real return. Your purchasing power does not increase. Equity at 12% provides approximately 6% real return after inflation.

Real return, not nominal return, determines wealth growth. Equity is the growth engine of long-term financial independence. Debt instruments provide stability and liquidity, but they rarely create substantial real wealth.

**Moral: Duration of investment with a higher return, magnifies the difference.**

## Staying Invested During Market Volatility

Understanding compounding mathematically is important, but living through volatility emotionally is equally critical. Most long-term wealth destruction does not happen because markets fail. It happens because investors interrupt compounding during temporary declines.

Look at the below given charts of the oldest Indian Stock Exchange (Sensex) and the oldest US stock exchange (DJI):

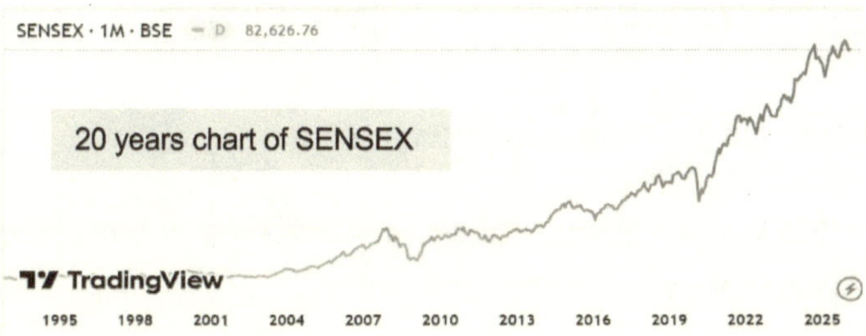


*Picture Credit: Trading View*

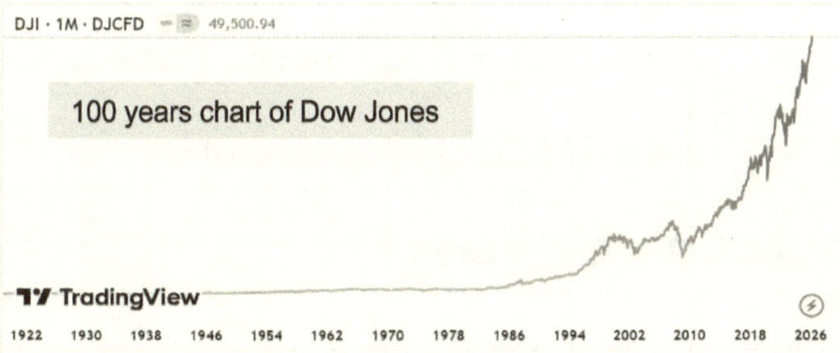


*Picture Credit: Trading View*

You can see volatility in the charts, with some big falls, yet the directions of both the indices are upward in the long run.

Market volatility is not an abnormal event. It is a structural feature of equity investing. Over any 20–25 year period, markets will experience multiple corrections of 15–20%, and at least a few deeper drawdowns of 30–40%. These phases are uncomfortable, but they are temporary.

Let us understand how systematic investing behaves during volatility.

Assume a monthly SIP of ₹10,000.

### Scenario 1 – Stable Market

If NAV (Net Asset Value) is ₹100 each month, the investor buys:

₹10,000 ÷ ₹100 = 100 units monthly.

After 12 months, total units accumulated = 1,200 units.

If NAV remains ₹100, total value = ₹1,20,000.

### Scenario 2 – Market Crash

Now assume the following pattern:

Months 1–6: NAV = ₹100
Months 7–12: NAV falls to ₹50

During first 6 months:

₹10,000 ÷ ₹100 = 100 units × 6 = 600 units

During next 6 months:

₹10,000 ÷ ₹50 = 200 units × 6 = 1,200 units

Total units accumulated after 12 months = 1,800 units.

Now assume market recovers and NAV returns to ₹100.

Portfolio value = 1,800 units × ₹100 = ₹1,80,000.

Total investment made = ₹10,000 × 12 = ₹1,20,000.

Even though the market ended the year at the same NAV of ₹100, the investor who continued investing during the crash accumulated more units and created ₹60,000 gain.

**This is rupee cost averaging** in action.

Market declines are not threats to SIP investors. They are discount periods.

The only condition is discipline.

If the investor had stopped SIP during the crash, he would have missed accumulating 1,200 units at lower prices. His long-term wealth would shrink significantly.

Volatility is not the enemy. Emotional reaction to volatility is the enemy.

## The Cost of Stopping SIP

Let us quantify the damage caused by interrupting compounding.

Assume:

Monthly SIP = ₹15,000
Return assumption = 12% annually
Investment duration = 20 years

If invested continuously for 20 years:

Future Value ≈ ₹1.5–1.6 crore

Total investment = ₹15,000 × 12 × 20 = ₹36 lakh

Corpus ≈ ₹1.5 crore

Now assume the investor stops SIP for 3 years during a market downturn between year 8 and year 10.

Effectively, he invests for only 17 years instead of 20.

Recalculated corpus ≈ ₹1.2–1.25 crore

Loss due to 3-year interruption ≈ ₹25–30 lakh.

Notice that he did not withdraw money. He simply paused contributions for three years. Yet the opportunity cost exceeded ₹25 lakh.

Why is the loss so large?

Because the contributions missed during mid-cycle growth years would have compounded for the remaining 10–12 years. When you stop investing, you do not merely skip contributions—you eliminate future compounding on those contributions.

Moreover, the years immediately following major crashes often deliver strong returns. If you pause during downturns, you miss recovery acceleration.

Historically, a small number of strong market recovery years contribute disproportionately to long-term returns. Missing those years significantly reduces final wealth.

Stopping SIP during downturn is equivalent to refusing to plant during the season right before the harvest.

## Why Consistency Beats Timing

Many investors believe they can improve returns by entering markets only when prices are "low." The challenge is that identifying the bottom in real time is nearly impossible.

No bell rings at market bottoms.

Let us examine a simplified illustration.

Suppose an investor remains invested in equity for 20 years and earns 12% annualized return.

Now assume another investor attempts to time the market and misses the 10 best-performing days over those 20 years.

Multiple studies globally have shown that missing just the 10 best days in long market cycles can reduce returns dramatically. For simplicity, assume that missing these best days reduces annualized return from 12% to 9%.

If ₹10 lakh is invested for 20 years:

At 12% annual return:
Future Value ≈ ₹96 lakh

At 9% annual return:
Future Value ≈ ₹56 lakh

Difference ≈ ₹40 lakh.

The only difference was missing a handful of best days.

Those best days often occur shortly after severe market declines—precisely when fearful investors remain on the sidelines.

Timing the market requires two correct decisions:

1. When to exit.
2. When to re-enter.

Getting both right consistently is extraordinarily difficult.

Salaried professionals have stable but limited income streams. Their competitive advantage is not market prediction. It is long-term consistency.

Time in the market allows compounding to operate fully. Timing the market interrupts it.

For salaried individuals, career growth should be the primary focus. Investing should run automatically in the background. Attempting to predict short-term market movements distracts from professional advancement and rarely improves long-term results.

## The 25-Year Discipline Model – Financial Independence Simulation

Let us now examine a structured long-term simulation.

**Assume:**

Monthly SIP = ₹20,000
Annual increase in SIP = 5%
Return assumption = 12%
Investment period = 25 years

The 5% annual increase accounts for salary growth and inflation.

Year 1 monthly SIP = ₹20,000
Year 2 = ₹21,000
Year 3 = ₹22,050
...and so on.

Using standard future value calculation for growing SIP at 12% return and 5% annual increase over 25 years:

Approximate corpus ≈ ₹4–5 crore (conservative midpoint: ₹4.5 crore).

Total contribution over 25 years would be significantly lower than corpus because compounding accelerates in later years.

Now consider withdrawal.

If this corpus of ₹4.5 crore generates 4% annual withdrawal:

4% of ₹4.5 crore = ₹18 lakh per year
₹18 lakh ÷ 12 ≈ ₹1.5 lakh per month

This becomes sustainable passive income, assuming prudent withdrawal rate and continued moderate growth of remaining corpus.

For an average salaried individual, ₹1–1.5 lakh monthly passive income is sufficient to maintain lifestyle in many cities, especially if home loan is cleared and children's education completed.

Notice what this scenario did not require:

- A lottery win.
- An inheritance.
- Speculative trading.
- Extraordinary business success.

Only:

- ₹20,000 disciplined SIP.
- Annual 5% increase.
- 25 years of patience.

This is financial independence achieved through structure and compounding. Time converts modest monthly discipline into substantial freedom.

## The Discipline Framework

Compounding is mathematical. Discipline is behavioral.

To protect compounding, follow these five golden rules:

1. Never stop SIP. Temporary discomfort must not interrupt long-term growth.

2. Never panic sell. Market volatility is normal. Selling during fear converts temporary decline into permanent loss.
3. Increase investment every year. Even a 5–10% annual increment significantly enhances final corpus.
4. Review annually, not daily. Daily monitoring magnifies emotion. Annual review preserves perspective.
5. Stay invested for minimum 10–15 years. Equity rewards long horizons. Short-term horizons convert equity into speculation.

These rules are simple but powerful. Wealth creation does not require complexity. It requires repetition.

## Emotional Stability and Wealth

Compounding rewards patience. Markets reward discipline.

Impatience destroys wealth not because returns are insufficient, but because investors interrupt the process prematurely.

Identity plays a critical role here.

If you see yourself as a trader, every fluctuation demands action.

If you see yourself as a long-term investor, fluctuations become background noise.

A salaried individual does not need market excitement. Stability of income combined with stability of investment process creates long-term growth.

The more emotionally detached you are from daily movements, the more powerfully compounding works.

Financial freedom is less about intelligence and more about emotional control.

## Transition to Financial Freedom Vision

Let us connect the journey so far.

In the first step we established Protection. Then we built Systematic Investing. And in this chapter, we learned Compounding.

**Protection prevents collapse.**
**Systematic investing builds assets.**
**Compounding multiplies assets.**

Together, they create freedom.

Freedom from EMI anxiety.
Freedom from retirement fear.

> Freedom to choose work rather than depend on it.

You do not need a high salary to achieve financial independence. You need disciplined investing, steady growth, and sufficient time.

Average earners become financially free not through extraordinary income, but through extraordinary consistency.

Compounding is patient. It does not rush. But it does not fail those who remain committed.

If you promise yourself one thing after reading this chapter, let it be this:

> You will not stop your SIP.
> You will not react emotionally to volatility.
> You will allow time to work.

Because time, when combined with discipline, becomes the most powerful wealth-building partner you will ever have.

# Chapter 9

# How to Apply: From Knowledge to Execution

## *Knowledge without Action is Useless*

Reading about wealth creation does not create wealth. Understanding compounding does not build a corpus. Knowing that insurance is important does not protect your family. Clarity without execution changes nothing.

Throughout this book, you have learned the structure: Protect → Invest Systematically → Multiply Through Compounding. You have now understood percentages, asset allocation, discipline, and long-term thinking. But unless these ideas are converted into action, they remain intellectual comfort.

Financial freedom is not achieved by motivation. It is achieved by installation of systems.

At this stage, your only responsibility is implementation. You do not need further theory. You do not need more YouTube videos. You do not need additional comparison research. You just need execution.

To eliminate confusion and procrastination, this chapter provides a structured **30-Day Financial Reset Plan, followed by a checklist**. If you follow the steps exactly as written, your financial life will be structurally transformed within one month.

You do not need to think. You only need to follow.

# The 30-Day Financial Reset Plan

This plan is divided into four weeks. Each week has a defined focus. Do not attempt everything on Day 1. Follow the sequence.

## Week 1 – Protection and Clarity

The objective of Week 1 is to secure the foundation.

**Step 1: List out Cash Inflow and Cash Outflows**

The first step toward financial freedom is clarity. List all sources of income, including bonuses, and convert them into a monthly figure. You must know exactly how much you earn before you build wealth. Next, divide your expenses into two categories: Essential (groceries, utilities, EMIs, rent, education, and other unavoidable costs) and non-essential (food delivery, OTT subscriptions, impulse spending, and lifestyle upgrades).

This simple exercise reveals how money comes into your life—and where it quietly goes.

**Step 2: Review Existing Life Insurance Policies**

Use the worksheet provided in chapter "Step 1 Protect: Building the Financial Foundation". Determine your required term cover based on income replacement, liabilities, and future obligations. Do not guess. Write down the number clearly.

List all current life insurance policies. Identify whether they are term plans or traditional savings-linked plans. Do not mix insurance and investment. You may exit the traditional life insurance plans, do not remain emotionally attached.

**Step 3: Purchase Adequate Term Insurance (If Required)**

Choose a reputable insurer. Ensure coverage equals at least 15–20 times your annual income or as per detailed calculation. Choose tenure up to planned retirement age or as per your requirement. Refer to the worksheets given in chapter 6 '*Step One-Protect: Building the Financial Foundation*'.

**Step 4: Purchase Personal Health Insurance**

If you rely only on employer coverage, purchase a personal policy immediately. Minimum coverage should align with age and income guidelines discussed earlier. Add a super top-up if necessary. Refer to the worksheets given in chapter 6 'Step One-Protect: *Building the Financial Foundation*'.

**Step 5: Open a Separate Emergency Fund Account**

Choose a bank different from your salary account. This reduces temptation. Transfer an initial amount toward emergency corpus.

**Step 6: Calculate Emergency Fund Requirement**

Determine your essential monthly expense accurately, see step 1 above. This number defines your emergency fund requirement and investment discipline. Refer to the worksheets given in chapter 6 '*Step One-Protect: Building the Financial Foundation*', to know your exact required amount of emergency fund.

Goal of Week 1: Your foundation is secured. You know your numbers.

## Week 2 – Build the System

Week 2 installs the wealth machine.

**Step 1: Open a Dedicated Investment Account**

This account will receive automatic transfers from your salary account. It must not be used for expenses.

**Step 2: Set Up Automatic Transfer**

Fix a standing instruction from salary account to investment account. If salary is credited on the last day of the month, set auto-transfer on the 2nd of the following month.

**Step 3: Decide Investment Percentage**

Write the percentage clearly. Commit to it. Refer to Chapter "Step 2: Invest Systematically: Turning Salary into a Wealth Machine".

**Step 4: Start SIPs**

Select funds based on your asset allocation model. Do not overcomplicate. 2–4 diversified funds are sufficient for most salaried individuals. Activate auto-debit SIP.

**Step 5: Stop Unnecessary Insurance-Investment Products**

Review endowment or money-back plans. If continuation makes no financial sense, plan phased exit. Avoid emotional attachment.

**Step 6: Create Simple Expense Tracker**

Track only categories, not micro-details. Housing, food, utilities, transport, discretionary. This helps control lifestyle inflation.

Goal of Week 2: System installed. Automation activated.

## Week 3 – Clean Financial Leaks

Wealth creation accelerates when financial leaks are sealed.

**Step 1: List All Debts**

Document home loan, car loan, personal loans, credit card balances.

**Step 2: Close High-Interest Credit Cards**

If outstanding credit card balance exists, prioritize repayment. Interest rates of 30–40% destroy compounding.

**Step 3: Stop Unused Subscriptions**

Streaming services, unused memberships, auto-renewing services. Small leaks compound negatively.

**Step 4: Avoid New Loans**

No new personal loans for lifestyle upgrades. No borrowing for gadgets. No impulsive EMIs.

**Step 5: Identify Lifestyle Inflation**

Compare current expenses with last year's. Has spending increased without proportional benefit? Adjust.

Goal of Week 3: Obstacles removed.

## Week 4 – Stabilize and Automate

Final week ensures durability.

**Step 1: Confirm All Standing Instructions Working**

Check that salary transfer, SIP auto-debit, and emergency contributions are functioning.

**Step 2: Increase SIP Slightly (If Possible)**

Even ₹1,000 increment reinforces discipline.

**Step 3: Allocate Increment Wisely**

If salary revision occurred recently, apply 50% increment to investments rule.

**Step 4: Write Long-Term Goals Clearly**

Retirement corpus target. Children's education target. Home loan closure timeline.

**Step 5: Final Cash Flow Review**

Ensure that post-investment balance covers expenses comfortably.

Goal of Week 4: System running without friction.

At the end of 30 days, your wealth structure is active.

# 30-Day Financial Reset Checklist

## Week 1 – Protection & Clarity

## *(Foundation Week)*

**This week is about securing your base. Do not rush. Complete each step carefully.**

### Life Insurance

☐ Calculated required life insurance using income replacement method
☐ Required cover amount written clearly: ₹ ______
☐ Existing policies reviewed
☐ Identified gap between required and existing cover
☐ Purchased / applied for pure term insurance
☐ Tenure chosen till retirement age or till the time all your financial liabilities are paid off
☐ Nominee details updated, informed the nominees about your insurance polices
☐ Policy documents stored safely (physical + digital)

### Health Insurance

☐ Verified employer coverage amount
☐ Purchased personal health insurance policy
☐ Coverage amount (₹15–25 lakh minimum)
☐ Super top-up added (if required)
☐ Family members covered
☐ Policy renewal date noted in calendar

### Emergency Fund

☐ Opened separate emergency fund bank account
☐ Calculated monthly essential expenses: ₹ _______
☐ Emergency fund target (6 months): ₹ __________
☐ Initial amount transferred: ₹ __________

### Financial Clarity

☐ Listed all monthly expenses
☐ Listed all EMIs
☐ Listed all loans outstanding
☐ Calculated current net worth (Assets – Liabilities)

### Week 1 Goal Achieved?

☐ Yes – Foundation secured
☐ Partially – Complete pending tasks before moving to Week 2

## Week 2 – Build the System

***(Installation Week)***

### This week is about building automation. No emotion. Only structure.

**Bank Structure**

☐ Opened separate Investment Account
☐ Confirmed salary credit date
☐ Set automatic transfer date (2nd of month or fixed date)
☐ Auto-transfer amount fixed: ₹ __________
☐ Investment percentage decided: _______%

**Investment Setup**

☐ Defined asset allocation (Equity …%/ Debt…..%)
☐ Selected mutual funds (2–4 maximum)
☐ Started SIP via auto-debit
☐ SIP start date confirmed
☐ Emergency fund contribution scheduled

**Remove Inefficient Products**

☐ Reviewed traditional insurance policies
☐ Identified policies to discontinue or make paid-up
☐ Avoided new insurance-investment products

## Expense Tracking

☐ Created simple expense tracker
☐ Defined monthly expense limit
☐ Set spending boundaries for discretionary expenses

## Week 2 Goal Achieved?

☐ Yes – System installed

☐ Adjustments required (Specify):

Notes________________________________________

______________________________________________

______________________________________________

______________________________________________

______________________________________________

______________________________________________

______________________________________________

______________________________________________

______________________________________________

______________________________________________

______________________________________________

______________________________________________

## Week 3 – Clean Financial Leaks

*(Stability Week)*

**This week removes obstacles that slow compounding.**

### Debt Management

☐ Listed all credit card dues
☐ Cleared outstanding credit card balances
☐ Stopped EMI-based lifestyle purchases
☐ No new personal loan taken
☐ Home loan EMI within safe limit

### Expense Optimization

☐ Cancelled unused subscriptions
☐ Reduced avoidable recurring expenses
☐ Identified lifestyle inflation areas
☐ Avoided impulse purchases

### Risk Control

☐ No F&O or speculative trading
☐ No tip-based investing
☐ No borrowing to invest
☐ No frequent fund switching

**Week 3 Goal Achieved?**

☐ Yes – Financial leaks sealed
☐ Pending actions (Specify):

Note________________________________________

## Week 4 – Stabilize & Automate

*(Automation Week)*

## This week ensures everything runs without constant supervision.

### Automation Check

☐ Salary auto-transfer executed successfully
☐ SIP deducted successfully
☐ Emergency fund contribution active
☐ Investment account functioning properly

### Improvement & Adjustment

☐ Increased SIP (if possible)
☐ Applied 50% increment rule (if salary increased)
☐ Reconfirmed investment percentage commitment
☐ Emergency fund progress reviewed

### Goal Clarity

**☐ Retirement goal written**
Target Corpus: ₹ __________
Target Retirement Age: ______

**☐ Children's education goal written**
Target Corpus: ₹ __________

☐ **Loan-free target year written: ______**

**Review System Installed**

☐ Fixed monthly 30-minute review date: ..................
☐ Fixed annual review date: ....................................
☐ Calendar reminders set

**Week 4 Goal Achieved?**

☐ Yes – System running automatically
☐ Minor adjustments pending

Notes________________________________________________

________________________________________________

________________________________________________

________________________________________________

________________________________________________

________________________________________________

________________________________________________

________________________________________________

________________________________________________

________________________________________________

__________________________________________

## Final Commitment Page

### After completing all four weeks:

☐ I have installed my financial system.
☐ I will not stop my SIP during market falls.
☐ I will increase investments every year.
☐ I will avoid emotional decisions.
☐ I commit to 20–25 years of discipline.

**Signature:** ______________________________

**Date:** ____________________________________

# 12-Month Financial Progress Tracker

Use this tracker to review your financial discipline every month. Tick the boxes after verifying completion during your monthly review.

| Month | Investment Done (SIP Active) | Emergency Fund Maintained | No New Debt Created | Monthly Review Completed |
|---|---|---|---|---|
| January | ☐ | ☐ | ☐ | ☐ |
| February | ☐ | ☐ | ☐ | ☐ |
| March | ☐ | ☐ | ☐ | ☐ |
| April | ☐ | ☐ | ☐ | ☐ |
| May | ☐ | ☐ | ☐ | ☐ |
| June | ☐ | ☐ | ☐ | ☐ |
| July | ☐ | ☐ | ☐ | ☐ |
| August | ☐ | ☐ | ☐ | ☐ |
| September | ☐ | ☐ | ☐ | ☐ |
| October | ☐ | ☐ | ☐ | ☐ |
| November | ☐ | ☐ | ☐ | ☐ |
| December | ☐ | ☐ | ☐ | ☐ |

# Chapter 10

# Method to Make ₹100 Crore through Salary - A Case Study

***Grow wealth slowly, like a forest — strong, silent, and lasting.***

Let us walk step by step through the journey of **Shri Rohit Kapoor** — not a businessman, not a startup founder, not a trader — just a salaried professional with clarity, discipline, and a long time horizon, how he made ₹100 crore from his salary.

Rohit Kapoor loved reading books. Not fiction alone, but biographies, investing classics, and stories of people who built wealth slowly. He came from a small town in Bihar. His family background was simple, middle-class, financially careful but not financially strategic. During his final year of college, one thought kept coming back to him:

He would often ask his teachers and friends:

> "Can a salaried person ever build ₹100 crore?"

Most people smiled sarcastically.

"Salary wale log ameer nahi bante." "If you want to be rich, start a business."

But Rohit knew one thing clearly.

His family situation did not allow him to take the risk of starting a business. He needed stability. He needed a salary.

So he asked himself a different question:

> "*If business is not an option, can I use my salary intelligently*?"

That question became his obsession.

## The Beginning – ₹60,000 Per Month

Soon after graduation, Rohit secured a job in an IT company in Bengaluru. His in-hand salary was ₹60,000 per month.

Not extraordinary.
Not poor.
Just average.

When he boarded the train from Bihar to Bengaluru, that same thought was in his mind:

"How can I retire with ₹100 crore?"

He slept in the train dreaming about that number.

When he woke up, the train had reached Bengaluru.

Life had begun.

## Smart Start in a Costly City

His office was in Whitefield.

Instead of renting a flashy apartment, Rohit chose a shared PG accommodation near his office. Rent including food: ₹12,000 per month.

Because the office was walking distance, he avoided auto and cab expenses.

Lifestyle was simple.

But the goal was big.

Here is how his first month's structure looked:

| **Expense Head** | **Amount (₹)** |
|---|---|
| PG + Food | 12,000 |
| Emergency Allocation | 8,000 |
| Term Insurance Premium | 1,180 |
| Super top up plan + Accident Insurance | 900 |
| Total Fixed & Protection | 22,080 |

Amount remaining from ₹60,000 = approx. ₹38,000.

Now observe something powerful.

As soon as his first salary credited, Rohit:

✔ Bought ₹1 crore term insurance
✔ Purchased super top up plan of health insurance of ₹15 lakh with ₹2 lakh deduction.
✔ Purchased accident insurance

Why?

Because he understood one principle:

> ***Wealth building without protection is incomplete.***

## The Calculator Moment

With ₹38,000 surplus, Rohit opened a retirement calculator.

Target: ₹100 crore
Time: 39 years (age 21 to 60)
Expected return: 13%
Annual step-up: 10%

Required monthly investment: **₹30,600**

He checked the number again.

₹30,600 was possible.

So he structured it.

He invested in three direct mutual funds.

₹10,200 in each.
Total SIP: ₹30,600 per month.

After everything, he still had ₹7,000 for discretionary expenses.

He did not feel deprived. He felt powerful.

For the first time, his money had direction.

## How ₹30,600 became ₹100 crore?

Let us simplify the mathematics.

Initial Monthly SIP: ₹30,600
Annual Investment: ₹3,67,200
Annual Step-up: 10%
Return Assumption: 13%
Duration: 39 years

Now understand something very important.

Compounding is not dramatic in the beginning.

**Phase 1: Foundation (Years 1–10)**

Corpus grows slowly.
People may laugh at you.
You may doubt yourself.

**Phase 2: Acceleration (Years 11–20)**

Growth becomes visible.
Returns start exceeding contributions.

**Phase 3: Explosion (Years 21–39)**

Compounding dominates.
Annual growth becomes massive.
Final 8–10 years create extraordinary wealth.

By year 39, this disciplined structure reaches approximately **₹100 crore**.

Not because of:

Trading
Crypto
Luck
Insider knowledge

But because of:

Annual increase in contribution
Staying invested in market crashes
No withdrawals
Long-term compounding

The early years built foundation.
The middle years built momentum.
The last decade built magnitude.

## Automation – The Hidden Superpower

Rohit automated everything.

SIPs auto-debited.
Insurance auto-debited.
Emergency fund systematically built.

He removed decision fatigue. This gave him mental freedom, and he focused on work.

His focus in work also resulted into fruits, and in his second year, he received:

✓ 20% salary increment
✓ ₹1 lakh bonus

Did he upgrade his lifestyle?

No.

He followed his plan.

He increased SIP by 10%.

The increment strengthened investments — not expenses.

That is the silent difference between dreamers and planners.

## What If He Delayed?

Now imagine Rohit delaying this by just 4 years.

If he started at 25 instead of 21:

Required monthly investment jumps from ₹30,600 to approx. ₹53,200.

Time is not a small variable.

Time is the biggest multiplier.

## The Core Lesson

Rohit did not start rich. He did not earn lakhs initially. He started with ₹60,000.

What made ₹100 crore possible?

- Early start
- Clear target
- Protection first
- Controlled lifestyle
- 10% yearly step-up
- 13% long-term compounding
- No interruptions

Nothing exotic. But, just structure.

## Now Let Us Talk About You

If you are 21 or 25, your advantage is time. But if you are 30 or 35, do not feel discouraged. Yes, ₹100 crore becomes difficult. But that does not mean financial freedom becomes difficult. It means the target must be recalibrated intelligently.

## The ₹50 Crore Strategy

If you are 30+ and reading this, you might feel regret.

“Why didn’t I start at 22?”

That feeling is natural. But regret does not build wealth.

Execution does.

Instead of ₹100 crore, target ₹50 crore.

Understand this clearly: ₹50 crore is not small. At 6% withdrawal rate, that generates ₹3 crore annually. That is ₹25 lakh per month without touching principal.

Is that a compromised life? Absolutely not. That is financial dignity.

## Required Monthly Investment for ₹50 Crore

Assumptions: Annual Return: 13%
Annual Step-up: 10%

**If retiring at 60:**

| Current Age | Starting Monthly SIP |
|---|---|
| 30 | ₹53,900 |
| 35 | ₹1,12,400 |

At first glance, this may look heavy.

If you want ₹50 crore, but the above monthly SIP amount appears scary to you, do not worry, I will give you a very good hack, where despite lower investments, you can achieve ₹50 crore target. Let's unveil the hack. -

# The 5-Year Compounding Hack

You do not have to retire at 60.

Extend retirement to 65.

Those extra 5 years dramatically reduce pressure.

Because the last 5 years of compounding are extremely powerful.

**If retiring at 65:**

| Current Age | Retiring at the age of 60, you need to start SIP with | Retiring at the age of 65, you need to start SIP with |
|---|---|---|
| 30 | ₹53,900 | ₹26,600 |
| 35 | ₹1,12,400 | ₹53,900 |

Notice the difference.

The dream remains ₹50 crore.

Only the timeline changes.

And suddenly, the target feels achievable. The SIP amount become half.

### Why This Works

Compounding curve is not straight. It bends upward sharply in later years.

By adding 5 more years:

- Your money works harder
- Your required SIP reduces
- Your psychological burden reduces

This is not lowering ambition. This is strategic intelligence.

## A Message to 30–45 Year Old Professionals

You are not late. Think what you have achieved, you have upper hand in your career, you must have got promotions or about to get one, you must be getting higher salaries than the fresher's, your EPF or PPF account must be having some balance.

If you commit to:

✓ 13% long-term growth target
✓ 10% annual investment increase
✓ No interruptions
✓ Staying invested in downturns

₹50 crore is absolutely achievable.

## The Emotional Shift

When you see ₹100 crore, you may feel intimidated. When you see ₹50 crore, you may feel hopeful.

When you see ₹26,600 per month, you feel it is actionable. That is the shift from fantasy to structure.

## Final Thought

Big wealth is not built by big income.

It is built by:

Big clarity.
Big patience.
Big discipline.

Rohit proved that salary is not a limitation. It is a platform. And now the question is not:

"Can a salaried person build wealth?"

The question is:

"Will you structure your salary intelligently?"

Because the day you convert your dream into:

- A number
- A timeline
- A return assumption
- A yearly step-up plan

Excitement replaces fear.

Hope replaces regret. And financial confidence begins.

The journey does not start with ₹100 crore.

It starts with your first structured SIP. And that can begin this month.

# Chapter 11

# The Middle-Class Money Trap

## *The Cost of Show-Off vs The Power of Compounding*

Public Provident Fund (PPF) is one of the most popular savings instruments among Indian middle-class families, especially salaried individuals. The tax benefits offered by the government, sovereign guarantee, and disciplined long-term structure make it an attractive investment option for conservative investors.

In this chapter, I will explain how you can extract the maximum benefit from your PPF account—what you should do and, more importantly, what you should avoid doing.

Let me introduce you to Girdhari Gupta, popularly known as GG Bhai among his friends.

GG Bhai started his career as a Probationary Officer in a reputed Public Sector Bank in January 2000. Like many young professionals, he believed that money was meant to be enjoyed. He lived life to the fullest, spending freely and enjoying the excitement of earning his own income.

In 2010, he was transferred to Mumbai. There, he noticed that many of his colleagues frequently discussed investments, retirement planning, and wealth creation. Gradually, he became interested in personal finance.

Inspired by his colleagues, GG Bhai made a New Year resolution. In January 2011, he opened a PPF account and started investing ₹12,500 every month without fail.

Fifteen years later, his disciplined investing habit was about to bear fruit.

His PPF account was due to mature that month.

His son, Girish, had already started making plans. He had convinced himself that once the PPF matured, the family would finally buy a luxury car.

One evening, Girish asked his father, "Papa, how much money has accumulated in your PPF account?"

GG Bhai smiled and replied, "The balance has grown to ₹39.45 lakh. Out of this, ₹22.50 lakh is the amount I invested, while ₹16.95 lakh is the interest earned."

Girish's eyes widened, ₹39.45 lakh!!

Until that moment, he had been dreaming of a ₹20 lakh car. Suddenly, he upgraded his dream to a ₹40 lakh luxury vehicle.

Excited beyond control, he immediately called his friends and invited them for dinner. He wanted to share the good news and discuss the new car he planned to buy next month.

That evening, all his friends gathered at a restaurant. Among them was Ravindra Jain, who worked with an investment bank.

As Girish enthusiastically described the features of the luxury car he intended to purchase, everyone seemed excited—except Ravindra. He remained unusually quiet and appeared busy on his phone.

Finally, Girish asked, “Ravindra, you don't seem excited. Don't you like the idea?”

Ravindra smiled and turned his mobile screen toward the group.

On the screen was a PPF calculator.

He entered the following figures:

- Current PPF Balance: ₹39.45 lakh
- Extension Period: 5 years

- Additional Investment: ₹0

The calculator displayed:

- Value After 5 Years: ₹55.60 lakh
- Growth in 5 Years: ₹16.15 lakh

The table fell silent.

Ravindra then asked, "Before deciding to buy the car, shouldn't we compare the alternatives?"

Everyone nodded.

He continued.

"If your father extends his PPF account for another five years and does not withdraw the money, the corpus will grow from ₹39.45 lakh to ₹55.60 lakh without any additional contribution."

Then he opened another calculator. This time he analysed the proposed car purchase.

### Scenario: Buying the ₹40 Lakh Car

- Purchase Price: ₹40 lakh
- Estimated Value After 5 Years: ₹16 lakh
- Depreciation Loss: ₹24 lakh
- Insurance and Maintenance Cost: ₹9.50 lakh

- Fuel Cost (Approximate): ₹6 lakh

The group looked shocked.

Ravindra explained calmly:

"If you buy the car today, ₹40 lakh immediately starts losing value. After five years, the car may be worth only ₹16 lakh. In addition, you would have spent approximately ₹15.50 lakh on insurance, maintenance, and fuel."

He paused for a moment.

"So the real comparison is not between owning a car and not owning a car. The comparison is between having an asset worth ₹16 lakh versus having a PPF corpus worth ₹55.60 lakh."

The difference was staggering.

The luxury car that seemed like a dream a few minutes ago suddenly looked very expensive.

But Ravindra was not finished.

He said, "Let's see what happens if your father not only extends the PPF but also continues investing ₹12,500 every month."

Once again, he entered the numbers.

- Current PPF Balance: ₹39.45 lakh
- Extension Period: 5 years
- Monthly Contribution: ₹12,500

The calculator showed:

**Value After 5 Years: ₹66.58 Lakh**

The growth over five years alone amounted to ₹27.13 lakh.

Girish could hardly believe what he was seeing.

“Wow! A growth of ₹27.13 lakh in just five years. That's unbelievable,” he exclaimed.

For the first time that evening, he began to understand the true power of compounding.

The conversation had completely changed direction.

A few hours earlier, everyone was discussing horsepower, leather seats, and alloy wheels.

Now they were discussing wealth creation.

Curious to see the long-term impact, Girish asked another question.

“What if Papa continues the PPF for ten more years?”

Ravindra entered the following details:

- Current PPF Balance: ₹39.45 lakh
- Extension Period: 10 years
- Monthly Contribution: ₹12,500

The result appeared on the screen.

**Value After 10 Years: ₹1.03 Crore**

The total growth over the next ten years would be approximately ₹63.55 lakh.

The entire group was stunned.

A few moments of silence followed.

Finally, Ravindra smiled and said:

"The rich don't become rich because they earn more. They become rich because they give their money time to grow."

He continued:

"Most people destroy compounding every time they receive a bonus, a salary increment, a maturity amount, or a windfall gain. They spend first and invest later. Wealthy people do exactly the opposite. They invest first and spend what remains."

Those words stayed with Girish. That night, he did not merely postpone the car purchase. He learned a lesson that would shape his financial future.

He realised that he could continue using his old Swift car for several more years. The desire to buy a luxury vehicle was driven not by necessity but by the urge to impress others.

The next morning, he dropped the idea of purchasing the car.

More importantly, he became curious about investing and wealth creation.

The story of Girish is not unique.

Every year, thousands of salaried individuals receive maturity proceeds from PPF accounts, fixed deposits, insurance policies, annual bonuses, or incentives. Before the money even reaches their bank account, they mentally allocate it toward a new car, a lavish vacation, expensive gadgets, or lifestyle upgrades.

Very few stop and ask:

*"What would happen if I simply gave this money more time?"*

The difference between financial struggle and financial freedom often lies in that one question.

Remember:

*People become temporarily happy by spending money.*

*They become permanently wealthy by allowing compounding to work.*

The next time you receive a large sum of money, think of Girish, GG Bhai, and Ravindra.

Before making a purchase, ask yourself: *Do I want temporary excitement, or do I want long-term wealth?*

Your answer may change your financial future forever.

# Acknowledgements

Writing a book is never a solitary effort. Though one name appears on the cover, many hearts stand behind the journey.

I am deeply grateful to my parents, whose values, sacrifices, and discipline laid the foundation of everything I have achieved.

To my wife, **Surbhi**—for her unwavering belief, patience, and constant strength. To my daughter, **Prisha**, and my son, **Reyansh**—you are the reason this book exists. Every lesson on financial security and freedom is inspired by my desire to build a stable and meaningful future for you.

My sincere thanks to the friends and mentors who enriched my thinking and helped shape the ideas in this book. A special thanks to my friend **Jay Nahata** for his valuable time and support in reviewing the manuscript.

Finally, thanks to every reader who has chosen to invest time in this book. I hope it helps you build not just wealth, but also confidence, responsibility, and lasting financial freedom.

**With gratitude,**
**Balram Chaudhary**

www.ingramcontent.com/pod-product-compliance
Lightning Source LLC
LaVergne TN
LVHW100305210926
848480LV00003B/1024